They Walked With Me

They Walked With Me

by Nimbilasha Cushing

ISBN 978-0-9890731-9-6

STORIES BY NIMBI
South Bend, IN
storiesbynimbi@gmail.com

Dedication

To my siblings who have gone before:
Lorraine, 1932–1980; Ed Roy, 1940–2000; Charles, 1937–2001,
and Landers, 1935–2012. And to my brother and sister, Jonathan
and Rosemarie, who still walk with me. I love you all. You are with
me always.

Acknowledgments

Many of the same people who supported me during the writing of Come This Way—There is an Exit continued to encourage me through the progression of They Walked With Me.

More than anyone, my sister Rosemarie was with me every step of the way. Jonathan, the only brother I have left, cheered me on whenever the opportunity presented itself.

At The Table, the writers group to which I belong, read and critiqued selected chapters. Thank you, Bonnie Bazata, Barbara Mangione, and Natalie Davis Miller.

Other readers included Christine Cushing, Linda Brookshire, Linda Lamar, Mary Reed, Sherry Marker, Sylvia Mischal, Sheila Jackson, Mike and Willye Bryan, Brian Dyde, John Raymer, Roxanne Lien, Loretta Wasmuth, Sally Wasmuth, Barbara Groner and Pamela Shafer Wycliff.

Some of you read a chapter and others read the entire manuscript. But the toughest critic of all, and the one whose approval I most needed, was my sister-friend, Barbara Mangione. Many thanks to Cheryl Reed, for getting the manuscript formatted.

Mary Marin, a gifted painter and friend, created the cover design.

Finally, to my love, James Langford, who took my calls at all hours and helped me consider the possibility that I was more than just an author. "You are a writer," he insisted and, at some point, I began to believe him.

I remain overcome by the extraordinary kindness and generosity of everyone mentioned here.

Prologue

In the winter of 2012, I self-published Come This Way—There is an Exit and offered it for consideration by the general public. The response to the copies now in circulation has been gratifying.

In that book, I told a story of intimacy. I tried to pay tribute to the people who raised me and gave me a strong foundation.

They Walked With Me continues the story of a little girl who started out as a sharecropper and ended up traveling the world.

While I have dedicated the book to my siblings, the love that I shared with my husband, James Cushing, has been at the core of all that I have written since his death in 2002. Jim and I had been married twenty-two years when life ended for him. He was sixty-five. Seven years before his death, I wrote and gave him a poem.

Nearly ten years later, his daughter, Christine, discovered the piece on an old floppy disc and asked if I would include it in my next book. I said yes.

Of a Love Like Ours,
WHAT DO THEY KNOW?

They were not there that Sunday when you surprised me at my job. They didn't see the blush on your yet untanned cheeks as you stood there hesitant, wondering if it had been a good idea after all. I exited last, suitcase in tow. Loved ones meeting loved ones had already departed when through the open door I darted. With a straight-ahead look, one more trip logged in my book, no time for nonsense, I was on my way.

Young and fit, my body showed no sign of the three-day course just run. It would have drained a lesser woman, but not me. My stride was long, fast and straight; ten minutes to my car, I would not be late. And then I saw you.

You might have been meeting any one of the fair-haired, chalky-skinned women, members of my crew. But your eyes found mine and suddenly my legs were like unfinished Jello—wobbly, unsure. Like a prize toy in the hand of a hopeful parent encouraging that first step, you held onto—yet offered—a brilliant bouquet of flowers at their peak. I moved awkwardly toward them—and you, my heart strong but fast, body trembling and weak.

You wore shorts and sandals daring to expose your beautifully carved and unscarred, ivory feet. So unlike mine. Perfect.

Of a love like ours, what could they know?

Later, though not much, I realized that you were indeed a prince from ages past. Had you just awakened from a century's sleep? Princes are only imaginary figures in the minds of adolescent girls and mid-life women, are they not? No wonder they stared at us each time you stood and held my chair while I, head bowed, hurried off to find the comfort room or any place away from their marred vision. How long would it take me to persuade you not to rise? How foolish of me to try. What the hell. Let them look 'til they were full enough to choke or the bile in their throats made them cry. You were above it all and with your inner strength did lift me to that place. "Ignore them, they don't count, take my arm, show your grace. Hand in hand, together we will go, just keep your eyes upon my face."

Of a love like ours, what can they possibly know?

Is it so unthinkable that a prince would choose a princess for a date, a mate, a wife? And if she happens to be a nigger-baby/colored-child/negro-teen/black-girl/African-American woman, so what? The winds of time blowing across their faces will smooth the furrows in their brows; erase the cynical twists of their mouths; clear the matter of fear and hate from their squinted eyes—maybe. For can one so taut, afraid, and blind ever know or hope to find a love like ours?

The joy of the pain of giving birth was never mine for what it's worth. So rest easy you self-appointed judges of humanity. The beautiful child that would have been will not decorate your bland, planned, mundane little cul-de-sac.

A kinder thing to let us be and face up to the reality, that narrow minds and hearts so cold may seldom grasp but never hold the things that make a love so bold. A love like ours.

Through the going of the years, many were the tears that you kissed from my cheek. More than once you sat by my bed, holding my hand, rubbing my head, until the crisis was spent. Opportunity and time came for an intellectual/cultural change, so across the ocean we went—for one year. There again you stood, protecting me from axe-scented words that might have cut me through. You took the part of shielding my heart, 'twas not I who caught the real sting of blows, not I, my love, but you.

Of a love like ours, what do they know? What do they know?

Nimbilasha Cushing
27 August, 1995

CHAPTER 1

An Education of Sorts

My mother died suddenly from heart failure at age thirty-seven. No one would blame my father for sending my younger sister Rosemarie (Sis) and me three hundred miles south to Eads, a small town in western Tennessee. The decision separated us from him and our five older siblings, but my maternal grandparents were better suited to care for us. I was three and Sis, eighteen months.

The white landowner, George Bragg, on whose property my grandparents lived, dictated the structural pattern of my education for the first nine years. When it was time to chop or pick his cotton, we headed to the fields instead of the schoolhouse. It was the rule and not the exception that colored (that's what we were called back then) children missed at least three months of school each year. That was the status quo and neither my grandparents nor any other colored sharecropper in the segregated South had recourse against that unwritten law. That's just the way things were.

In elementary school I learned the advantage of keeping a low profile. Two stern, no nonsense, veteran teachers ran the four-room schoolhouse that I attended in Shelby County, Tennessee. First through fourth graders all studied in the same room under the watchful eye of Miss Shaw. As rigid as she was, those in the four upper grades would look back on their time with her as almost relaxed.

Fess (short for professor) was more tyrant than teacher. If asked, he would identify himself as Professor Jones though he held no advanced degree. His response to the slightest hint of misbehavior was to seize the long switch he kept within arm's reach. On occasion, he was satisfied to simply raise the weapon above his head, waving it in a threatening manner in sync with a verbal warning.

But more often than not, some unlucky girl or boy would feel its sting, usually on bare legs if the girl wore a dress, or across the back, provided the boy's outer garments were thin enough for the lick to be felt.

Like any other kid at Wells Elementary who was paying attention, I soon learned how to avoid making myself a target of his discipline. My sister and I dreamed of a time when sharecropping would not dictate whether or not we attended school. The opportunity came when I was nearly fourteen. My father had remarried after being a widower for twelve years. He, along with our new stepmother, Beatrice, came to Tennessee and brought Sis and me back to

Saint Louis, the place where we were born. Neither of us was prepared for the sophisticated culture and lifestyle of up North city folks.

We arrived in St. Louis during summer vacation. After having our soon-to-be new school pointed out to me, I was petrified. The very size of the red brick building was daunting, and that was even before I saw the inside.

Soldan's two thousand students more than tripled the population of the town that had been my home the previous twelve years.

I enrolled as a sophomore in the fall of 1963 and graduated the spring of '66. My poor social skills and lack of style could have made me an easy target for bullying. But before ever passing through the doors into the building, I devised a plan that assured anonymity. I would be one of the faceless in its corridors, classrooms, and recreational areas. Display of any talents or character strengths might set me apart for potential ridicule rather than securing a place for me in a small group. The safety net was not to withdraw, but rather to never leave the cocoon in the first place. A page-by-page review of the yearbook will not reveal a single photograph of me though my name appears as a member of the graduating class. More than forty years later, I have yet to send or receive the first note from a classmate or be invited to a reunion.

Clark Elementary School was visible from our front

porch. A shortcut across its playground would get me from our house at 5219 Cabanne to the main entrance of the high school in fewer than ten minutes. I always made it there before the bell rang but not too early, for that would mean having free time to linger and possibly interact with other students.

Within the first few weeks, I came to view at least two teachers as allies should I need one. Miss Phillips taught English. Frequently before the onset of our workdays, she could be found reading a book while strolling back and forth along the corridor near the main office. She had the ability to keep one eye on her book while the other monitored everything that was going on around her.

"Sylvester," she would call, "shouldn't you be on your way to Mr. Brown's room? Why are you down here?"

If she called on you, you knew you were wrong, but she had an approachable manner and a love for teaching. Miss Phillips shared those traits with the student teacher of the same name who taught me when I was in third grade.

The first Miss Phillips was the most beautiful woman, colored or white, that I had ever seen. Tall already, she added to her height by wearing high heeled shoes with silk stockings almost every day. She was thin, but not skinny, and had satiny smooth, mocha colored skin. Her hair was similar to my own. Not what colored people called good but not totally *bad* either. Miss Phillips knew how to style it so that it was always in place and complimented her face. Impeccably dressed in flattering tight skirts and chic blouses, she might have just stepped off a fashion runway.

The second Miss Phillips was old enough to be the mother of the first, and her style of dress made her appear somewhat dowdy. With minimal attention, the thick, wavy, salt and pepper hair could easily have been her best physical asset. Instead, she seemed to have allowed it to dry without using a comb or brush.

Most of her dresses fell below her calves, stopping a few inches above her black, laced, but untied "old-lady comforts" (stacked heel shoes). She wore her nylon stockings rolled down so they rested on the mouth of each shoe. In the classroom, though, she was engaging but clearly not one to put up with inattentiveness from any student. Her lectures on nouns, adjectives, and verb conjugations were well thought out and delivered in a deliberate style that fit her perfectly.

She loved poetry and, though she did not teach English literature per se, students were occasionally called on to stand and read from T.S. Eliot or Emily Dickinson. A raised eyebrow or a lowering of her glasses was our sign that what she was about to say would show up on the next exam. A superb teacher, she was always available to answer a question or explain a concept before or after class if one hadn't quite gotten it the first time around.

Mr. Thomas is the only other teacher whose name

comes easily to me. He taught biology. All I can say about him for sure is that every girl in that school had a thing for him. He was fine and his clothes accented all his good features. He nearly always wore coordinating jackets and slacks but never a suit. He was about six feet tall with not an extra pound anywhere as best I could tell.

The thin mustache and sharply edged sideburns framed a pecan colored face that begged to be stroked. The dilemma of being in his class was deciding whether to study like crazy in hopes of getting special attention or purposely flunking the course in order to retake it from him the next school year.

A few years later when I saw Sidney Poitier in *To Sir with Love*, my mind returned to Mr. Thomas. He was the first man I'd known who walked with that smart, snappy swagger that causes women to stare. Had my tenth grade biology teacher served as the prototype for my favorite male actor or was it the other way 'round? As handsome as he was, no one felt intimidated by his good looks. Everyone knew that he was available and willing to spend extra time with a struggling student. I could have used the help but was too shy to ask.

My grandparents' role as guardians during my early childhood and into adolescence did not focus on building confidence or self-esteem. They demonstrated their love for me in words—"Big Mama loves you"—and actions that included giving lots of hugs and tickling me under my arms until I nearly peed in my pants. Nevertheless, the discourse did not generally include compliments on my looks or intellect. Instead, Sis and I were often told to "be good" but seldom that we *were* good.

My third grade student teacher, Miss Phillips, whom I thought of as being there only for me, did all that she could to make us believe in ourselves. It was not until many years later that I began to realize how important her influence had been in my life. When she left, however, I returned to operating in a mindset that tagged me as simple, unattractive, and "country." Those were the messages I internalized without question. My doubts and insecurities became self-fulfilling.

I learned from my stepmother Beatrice that studying hard was essential to success. A wretched creature most of the time, she sincerely loved knowledge. Beatrice read everything she could get her hands on, further affirming my opinion about the value of learning. She was consumed with the desire for one of her children, even a stepdaughter, to become a doctor, attorney, or teacher. She made herself available whenever one of us got stuck with a mathematical concept or, for that matter, any other homework that gave us difficulty. I have little enough to thank her for, but it was due to her help that I performed well enough to earn better than passing grades. I carried a B average all three years.

Outside the classroom setting, however, I kept to my original plan to maintain obscurity. It had not taken me long to figure out that labels such as the "in crowd" were as flimsy as the maroon and gold school color pom-poms showcased by popular cheerleaders. Whatever acceptance I might gain paled next to the ridicule I felt sure would come if ever I lowered my guard.

Our new home life was not one that we wanted to share with anyone who might befriend us. Except on rare occasions, our stepmother's rule prohibited us—and that included her own daughter Kiki—from inviting friends over after school or on weekends. Since I had none, the decree was an easy one to follow.

My shyness did not prevent me from having a huge but silent crush on a guy named Chester Stanton. His friends called him Chip, as did I, but only in private. I would look in the bathroom mirror and carry on brief one- way conversations with him almost every day. There is no reason for me to think that he ever had a clue about my feelings. No one did. What would have been the point of sharing such fantasies? On the other hand, how cool could a guy named Chester, with his thick, black-framed glasses, really be? Who's to say he didn't have similar feelings for me? Even if that were true, I doubt his parents would have approved of our being friends. For unlike my father and stepmother, Chip's parents were professionals. His dad wore a suit and tie to work while mine wore washable blue pants and a shirt with the sleeves rolled up during summer. Secretly daydreaming romantic scenes was safer than exposing myself to the mockery of the other girls.

I graduated in June of '66 and continued working the part-time job I had begun as a junior. Hospital work suited me, particularly in the area of food service. My responsibilities included loading large shelved carts with trays of food and transporting them to various floors. I longed to deliver the meals to the patients, but that job fell to another group of employees assisted by teams of candy stripers. I longed to be one of them and to wear the starched red and white pinafore. But this group of perky volunteers—all white—did not have to worry about a paycheck. The time would come when I would deliver countless trays of food wearing a much classier uniform. But that was still ahead.

My position at Barnes Hospital amounted to little more than filling a slot in a temporary holding pattern. Unbeknownst to my co-workers, I investigated the possibility of enlisting in the Air Force when I turned eighteen, six months after graduation. Three of my brothers had preceded me in military service though only one of them went voluntarily.

Charles enlisted in the Air Force at seventeen with our father's signed permission. Jonathan, who was older than Charles, and Ed Roy, who was younger, were both drafted into the Army. Perhaps not surprisingly, Charles seemed to have the more positive opinion of military life. He was ten years older than I and, as handsome as he was in civilian clothes, he was stunningly good looking in uniform. My admiration for him quite likely sparked the idea that Air Force life could work for me as well.

The recruiter who came to my school on career day was likely chosen for his duty, in part, because he was drop dead gorgeous. That day Mr. Thomas had some competition from an even taller black man whose good looks were not marred in the least by the gold-rimmed glasses he wore. If anything, they added a touch of maturity that made him even more desirable. His talk was way too short for me and I was thrilled that, of the twelve of us who had signed up for his presentation, there was only one other girl in the room.

When the session was over, she left without picking up a single flyer. I, on the other hand, took one of everything displayed on the small table. The smooth talking recruiter urged me to complete one of the forms that asked for basic information. He then looked me over and told me that he saw no reason I would not be accepted into service. "You are a little on the thin side. Use the summer to put on some weight. Eat all the White Castles and milkshakes that you want."

I finished filling in the form being careful not to make any mistakes, though I sensed a slight trembling in my hand.

In early fall when I went for my initial physical exam, I was informed that my weight of a hundred and twelve pounds still did not meet the minimum requirement for my 5'9" frame. By this time I was pulling eight-hour shifts at the hospital. One of the advantages of working in the kitchen was the availability of a tempting array of fattening foods. I would not have a problem putting on ten pounds, or so I thought. At first it was easy to fill up on roast beef, fried chicken, ham, baked beans, and mashed potatoes with extra butter followed by chocolate cake and ice cream. However, after a few weeks of marathon eating and gaining more facial zits than pounds, my delight in having as many desserts as I wanted waned considerably.

My work life was my social life. Our tasks were menial and easily mastered, and we all got along. Mabel was second in charge and did not tolerate "no bad attitudes in my kitchen." She was built like a female wrestler or maybe one of Jim Croce's roller derby queens. It would not have surprised me to learn that at some point she had done time. She wore a wig of soft black curls and a half bang. It was too small. She would hold the wig down with one hand while trying to stretch the mandatory hairnet over it with the other. Sometimes the wig shifted back exposing her own short brittle hair. This agitated her to no end, yet she refused help from anyone brave enough to offer. On that rare occasion when she smiled, any hint of meanness was wiped away with the parting of her full red lips. Underneath her armored exterior beat a tender heart. More than a few times, Mabel would bring in small plastic toys to place on some of the children's trays. She didn't seem to have a plan for which two or three kids would be the lucky ones on a given day and, of course, none of us questioned what she did.

Not until I was absolutely certain that Uncle Sam would take me did I tell my coworkers of my upcoming departure. It had not been easy to keep quiet about my plans. The looming possibility that I'd be turned down at the last minute was the only reminder I needed to remain discreet until I had passed all the written and physical exams.

On Thanksgiving we had drawn names to exchange inexpensive Christmas gifts. I drew Clara Jordan, whom we jokingly called Clara Barton after the famous nineteenth century nurse. The would-be Nurse Jordan was quick to make off-the-cuff diagnoses for anyone careless enough to complain of a headache, sore throat or scraped knee. I gave her a toy first aid kit that held a tiny thermometer, a couple of Band-Aids and a pretend bottle of aspirin. No one laughed harder than Clara when she unwrapped the small box.

Toward the end of our little party in the bowels of Barnes Hospital, a place that had been a refuge for me, I shared the news that I would be leaving. My friends— yes, they had earned that title—were amazed and full of questions. It was one of the few times I felt excited and proud to be the girl who had come from the country because I was now on the brink of taking a step forward— not just for myself, but for others like me.

CHAPTER 2

Learning the Basics

It was a cold day in February 1967 when I prepared, with some trepidation but no regret, to leave behind all that was familiar. The freezing temperatures bolstered my resolve to take one step and then another toward the new life that awaited me under a warm San Antonio sun. By the morning of my departure, I had come to terms with the initial disappointment I felt when I was given a train instead of an airplane ticket for the long trip. It was impossible to enter Union Station without momentarily being swept back in time to those rare early morning arrivals when Big Mama had brought Sis and me from Tennessee to St. Louis to visit Daddy and our five older siblings.

But this was different. I was about to take my very first solo train ride. The act of doing so elevated me to a different status. I was an adult about to set off into the unknown. My father was fearful for me. "My sons were in the military, but that is no place for my daughter."

My brothers also tried to dissuade me. At least two of them, one who had never been in service, were convinced that I'd be "attacked by lesbians and become one," as if sexual orientation were infectious like the measles. "You'll never survive," they said.

My stepmother Beatrice was angry and disappointed.

She saw all those hours of helping me with my homework as wasted effort. "You are wasting your life. You could have continued working, gone to college and gotten a degree. You like the hospital. If you couldn't be a doctor, you could have at least become a nurse or a teacher. But you chose to do this thing behind our back. I've had it with you."

All the while she was lecturing me, my thoughts were that I would soon be out of that house and away from her, wretched creature that she was.

But now, standing on that platform, I wanted nothing more than for Daddy to hug me and say, "Okay, that's enough of this nonsense. Let's go home." Daddy may have had the same thoughts going through his head, but just as when Rosemarie had left home and moved in with our brother Landers and his wife the year before, he showed no emotion. My arms ached to reach out and hold him—to switch roles for just that moment. I dared not.

Another part of me could hardly wait to hand my ticket to the uniformed conductor who stood a few feet to our right. Mercifully, Beatrice had not accompanied us but chose to say goodbye from the comfort of her warm bed.

That suited me fine. Our relationship had been stretched to the point that a lone tether connected us to one another. Her husband, my father, was that tenuous link. I hoped my leaving would prompt them to become reacquainted and settle into a state of mutual contentment. He, at least, deserved that.

Once in my seat I chose not to look out the window. I didn't know if Daddy would still be standing there or not. If he were, the sight of him would have pumped out tears that I was determined to keep in their reservoir until the train was moving.

More than thirty hours later I disembarked to be greeted by the hissing sound of steam escaping from the long locomotive. The crowded train, as it turned out, had been a pleasant space to share with a group of strangers I would never see again. After about a minute, I realized that I had stopped in the middle of the platform. Passengers began bumping into me or saying "excuse me" as they stepped to one side or the other to get by.

"Welcome to San Antonio," the large, colorful sign seemed to shout. It didn't take long before I noticed three other individuals looking as lost as I felt. Nothing the recruiter might have said earlier could have prepared me for the momentary panic that took hold of me.

I approached the two guys and one girl and asked if they were waiting to be met by Sergeant Miller. Indeed they were, and I breathed easier knowing that I was now one of a small cluster, no longer alone. We started chatting and pretty soon a young man in a khaki colored uniform and navy-blue hat approached us. He was carrying a single manila folder that he opened to scan the papers inside. His greeting was friendly and informal.

"Good afternoon. I'm Staff Sergeant Jason Miller. Welcome to Texas and Lackland Air Force Base."

The perfunctory salutation out of the way, it was on to business. Sergeant Miller read off our names and serial numbers in a precise, metered tempo. My recruiter had instructed me to memorize the serial number even if that meant forgetting my name. I was Airman (not Airwoman) Basic Harris, Mary Alice, AA26891507. If I survived the next six weeks, I would get to drop the *Basic* and become simply Airman. But I had not yet earned that privilege. In short order it became apparent to anyone paying attention that those of us in the Airman Basic category had no place on the totem pole of Air Force hierarchy; rather we were the dirt in which the pole was planted.

The first few days in a new and different world passed in a blur. Everything that had been done in St. Louis through my recruiter and his staff with regard to establishing my physical condition had to be repeated. We filled out the same batch of papers we had submitted months earlier.

The next step was to get fitted for uniforms. As WAF (Women's Air Force), we received three styles: green fatigues, work blues and dress blues. We wore fatigues for some physical fitness training and for the messier work details. Most of us wore work blues for our everyday assignments. We had two choices. One was a light blue striped seersucker skirt with short sleeve jacket. I preferred the second choice, the washable light blue shirt and navy-blue trousers because I was embarrassed by my skinny legs. I worked at the base education office as a receptionist. My duties included handling the phone calls, typing, filing, and sometimes running errands for the office manager.

Hats were a mandatory part of the uniform when outdoors. The hat we wore most often could be folded flat and carried easily. Some of us called it the envelope. When opened, it was an easy fit for the men with their close cut hair, but women had to anchor it down with bobby pins.

Dress blues were reserved for special occasions such as parades when distinguished guests were on base and for ceremonies on Memorial, Independence, and Veteran's Day. That outfit consisted of a dark blue suit with a light blue shirt worn underneath the long sleeved jacket.

Sergeant Imler had the task of shaping us into airmen worthy of wearing that respected Air Force blue. She seldom missed a chance to remind us of the tough challenge that had fallen to her. Because, as she put it, we were, "the sorriest excuse of women recruits I have ever laid eyes on.

But the United States Air Force is counting on me to make something out of nothing, and I will not let them down."

We heard that speech or a variation of it every day for the first two weeks of training. Failing in this new arena was not an option for me. I decided the moment I passed through the gate onto the sprawling base that I would not return to St. Louis, Missouri, or Eads, Tennessee, except in uniform—the Air Force uniform.

Sergeant Imler was from Oklahoma, the backbone of the whole nation, according to her. She spoke in a high-pitched voice that was made more unpleasant by the fact that she shouted every directive she ever issued, even when standing within two feet of her subject. She must have barely met the minimum height requirement, which I believe was five feet even. Her short, dark, auburn hair looked as if she had fallen asleep while waiting for the Lilt Foam Perm to take affect. The envelope-shaped hat perched on top of her head only increased our temptation to laugh as corkscrew curls sprang out from under it in every direction. But none of us was dumb enough to do that, at least not in her presence.

I never witnessed the woman strolling casually from one point to another. Instead, she marched as if on an important mission, as if the burden that had been placed on her shoulders demanded that she make the most of every minute. She stretched her legs to their limit by taking long strides indoors and out. When in our barracks we were able to hear her approach long before we saw her as she pounded her heels into the shiny-waxed floors." "

It was possible, though unlikely, that we could have gone almost anywhere in the world after basic training. Given the number of inoculations they gave us, we might have been shipped to the rain forest of the Amazon or the deepest jungles of Africa.

Lined up in rows of eight, we rolled up our sleeves baring upper arms "in order to expedite the process." Two medics would approach, one carrying the tray of needles and the other administering the prescribed injection for the day. Sergeant Imler informed us that, "You will not faint." Anyone who did so would be deprived of one of our few meager privileges or given some type of extra duty. Some fainted, but I never did.

I did learn to cry without uttering a sound. The tears that rolled down my cheeks the first few times were of relief that I was left standing after the stinging attack to my skinny arm.

Prior to swearing me in to active duty, my recruiter had instructed me to gain ten pounds. At the final weigh in, he placed his large foot on the scale while I was standing on it. The physician recording the numbers pretended not to notice. I was five nine and weighed one hundred and sixteen pounds. Even with all the extra calories I consumed while working in the hospital, I still arrived at Lackland Air Force Base four pounds under the required minimum weight for my height. But at that point I was in, and there was no danger of anyone sending me home for being too skinny.

Our barracks were inspected three times a week, excluding Saturday and Sunday. On those days we could actually make our beds pretty much as we liked. But Monday through Friday the linens on each bed had to be stretched tight enough so that, if Sergeant Imler chose your bed to do the quarter test, the coin would bounce. She did not check all thirty-two beds in my barracks, but if any one bed was made inadequately, everyone paid a price. The strategy produced the outcome she desired. We worked together combining our strengths in order to eliminate our weaknesses. Our sergeant was forging friendships while pretending to find us nearly intolerable.

Training escalated by increments. As we became proficient in one set of skills, the next demanded even more from us. We dared not grumble. Anyone who outranked us had the right to remind us that we represented something far greater than ourselves. They never missed that opportunity—even if they had only one stripe on their uniform and even if they had sewn on that one stripe the day before.

We were identified by the word *Flight* followed by a number. The number coincided with how many groups of trainees were ahead of ours that year. My group of thirty-two was Flight Eight comprised of five blacks, one Puerto Rican, and the rest white. I managed better than most of the other girls primarily because I was quick to rise. While they were pulling the covers over their heads and swearing at the bugler for sounding reveille before daylight, I would already be in the bathroom. There were not enough showers for everyone to use them at once. Stragglers ended up waiting in line for a sink or shower stall to become available.

I went into the shower geared with everything I needed including toothbrush and paste. When I emerged, I needed only to dry off and get dressed. The uniform of the day was always announced at least a day in advance taking all the guess work out of what to wear. I prided myself on arriving early at the mess hall or anywhere else when group movement was not required. Sergeant Imler placed a check mark next to our names as we stepped smartly past her.

Anyone arriving two minutes late would not get breakfast that day. Eating well became an essential of daily life in order to perform at the levels demanded; it did not take long for me to gain the necessary four pounds.

Physical exercise and marching were part of our daily routine, and evenings were spent studying for weekly exams. AFSC stands for Air Force Specialty Code. It contains five numbers. The first three designate the field or occupation and the last two, the level of competence.

As an administrative specialist, my numbers were 70210. Part of that first six weeks in service included classes in typing, filing, telephone etiquette, a condensed version of shorthand and learning to operate various models of copy machines. A successful grade upped the last two numbers. I left Lackland Air Force Base as a 70230.

Once we passed the halfway mark of our training period, Sergeant Imler occasionally counted the marching as our exercise for that day, giving us a free hour. Depending on the time, most girls ran to the day-room to try and catch their favorite soap opera. I headed for my bunk to seize the rare opportunity of a nap.

In the third week of training, a special unit comprised entirely of exceptionally handsome men paid a visit to our base. They were members of the Honor Guard from Bolling Air Force Base in Washington, D.C. They could march better than any group of men I'd ever seen. But then, that was their job: Honor Guards. That pretty much said it all. One guy caught my eye. In fact, unless there was a blind woman on the base, we were all checking him out.

In any event, a group of WAFs were uninvited spectators. When he passed near where we stood, I thought he was looking right at me. To my delight, he came over after the procession was finished and asked me if I wanted to go to the Service Club for a coke. I pondered the idea for about a millisecond before saying, "Uh sure," or some such dimwitted reply. We walked away and I could feel the daggers being thrown into my back by my comrades. I held my head up all the higher and took a sidestep that caused our bodies to touch. I was surprised at my brazenness. Slowly and by degree, the shy girl from the country appeared to be transforming into someone else.

His name was Jerome Henderson, a tall guy with broad shoulders, smooth mahogany skin, and stately posture. If he'd noticed the shift of my body against his own, he did not let on.

As we continued walking unhurriedly, Jerome told me that in the fourth week of basic training I would be given the opportunity to request where I wanted to be stationed. He asked me to consider requesting his base but quickly added that he had only a year remaining of his four-year term.

What can I say? I was eighteen and gullible. Why else might I have imagined that such a prize of a guy had been twiddling his thumbs waiting around to meet a girl like me? Then again, my transformation had only begun. The finished product might turn out to be someone even I could not recognize.

We had only thirty minutes together before I had to report for some stupid detail. We exchanged addresses and promised to write to each other. I practically skipped back to the barracks to change into my fatigues. Thank goodness we had not been wearing them earlier in the day. They were the least flattering of all the uniforms.

The next week we were given yet another set of forms to complete. Among them was the one I was looking for. We were asked to list three places we'd like to be stationed. The needs of the Air Force came first, but consideration to our preferences would be given when possible. I was tempted to list Washington on all three lines. Instead, I wrote it in as my first choice. California was next and, finally, Missouri. When the list of assignments was posted, my heart momentarily stopped. I found my serial number and next to it the word Washington, McChord Air Force Base. McChord—not Bolling. I had gotten my first choice all right but, to my dismay, it would land me 2500 miles from where I wanted to be. In my eagerness to complete the form, I had not written the letters D.C. after Washington.

That night I wrote my third letter to Jerome telling him of my fate. He had only written to me once anyway, and that was in the form of a post card with a picture of the White House on the front. I neither heard from nor saw him again.

We were required to write at least one letter a week to family back home. Before we mailed it, our sergeant did a visual check to verify that we had neatly written at least a page. Despite a tough exterior, she cared about us and, at the end of six weeks, many of us were sad to say good-bye to her.

Completing basic training gave me a sense of pride of accomplishment that I had not previously known. The training was physically rigorous and mentally challenging. But, thanks to the work ethic I had learned as a child, having endured all those sweltering days in the cotton fields, I had not only survived the six weeks but had come through with an element of dignity and grace. I would build on that.

I never again saw any of the women from my Flight, nor Sergeant Imler. In a different way she had given me an added dose of what my third grade teacher poured into me years before. My beloved teacher, Miss Phillips, had taught me to dream. Sergeant Imler instilled in me the knowledge that any worthwhile dream comes at a cost.

CHAPTER 3

Proud to Wear the U.S. Air Force Blue

The first time I flew over the area surrounding Seattle–Tacoma (Sea-Tac) Airport, my mind could not immediately take in its majestic beauty. The approach over the Cascades and Mount Rainier, studded with evergreens that seemed to be kissing the sky, and the sparkling waters of Puget Sound gave me a feeling that I was finally home. By the time we parked at the gate, I had decided that I would never live anywhere else.

As I approached the baggage claim area, another airman raised his hand to get my attention. He had already met the sergeant who would usher us through the next phase of Air Force life. Sergeant Christopher Bower explained that we needed to wait for another flight carrying five more transferees. They were coming from McGuire AFB in New Jersey. When everyone was gathered, I was the only Airman Third Class in the group and the only female. Still, I was proud of that single stripe on the arm of my uniform jacket. It meant that I had survived what I hoped would be the toughest part of my time in service.

Everyone else in the group had completed at least two years active duty and had the stripes to prove it. An Airman Second Class had two stripes, an Airman First Class had three, and a Staff Sergeant had four. At least that's how it was in 1967. Once we all loaded into the van, I forgot to be nervous about being the only female, and rank ceased to matter once I was invited to sit up front with Sergeant Bower.

He told us that the ride would take forty-five minutes. In short order we were headed south toward Tacoma. Before ever touching the ground, I had prayed for a much longer drive to the base. The magnificent trees visible from the air now stretched along each side of Interstate 5. I had never seen trees as tall and thick as the ones lining the roadway.

I leaned forward trying to see upward through the windshield. For a moment the thought entered my head to ask if we could stop long enough to take one picture, but good sense overruled the impulse and I kept my mouth shut. Getting out of the van for even a minute might have resulted in losing my seat to one of the guys who now wished he hadn't been so chivalrous when we were loading up. Besides, since this was going to be my home for, I thought, the rest of my life, I would have plenty of time to explore it at my leisure.

When we reached McChord Air Force Base, some forty miles south of Seattle, I remained spellbound—for three years. I never ceased to be amazed by the natural splendor of the place even when it rained for days at a time. My four years in the military remain the period of my life with the fewest regrets.

Soon after we were waved through the main gate of the base, our first stop was WAF headquarters. It was in the middle of the afternoon. Several young women in civilian clothes were milling about. They turned out to be among the many who worked nights and had their days free. I got out of the van and said good-bye to the guys almost as an afterthought. My focus on the inescapable beauty of the area had blocked out everything else. Surely conversation must have taken place during the ride, but it had been lost on me.

The first woman I met at McChord was Sergeant Kennedy, the administrative assistant to the WAF Squadron commander. She smelled like an ashtray badly in need of cleaning.

I guessed that she had started smoking about the time she was in middle school. The smell permeated the large open pores on her face. The pockets beneath her eyes were probably filled with smoke she had inhaled and was saving for a time when she might not have a cigarette handy. Her fingernails, yellowed by the nicotine, were evidence of the fact that she left very little—if anything— to be snuffed out. Her hair seemed in need of a good shampooing, and the smoker's cough was no longer an inconvenience to her. If she started to cough while speaking, she did not pause. It was up to the listener to figure out what in the world she had said.

At least one room separated Master Sergeant Kennedy's office from her boss. While every window in the Sergeant's office was open, the doors between the two offices were kept closed.

Captain Rutledge, a tall, stocky blonde, was the second woman I met at McChord. She stood up when her administrator brought me into her office. I remembered to salute mostly because the sergeant had reminded me seconds earlier. The Captain spent about ten minutes with me. She asked about my flight and I responded with perhaps too much detail, including that it had been my first. "And what did you think of basic training? Did you enjoy that too?"

"Yes, ma'am," I lied. I thought a moment and then gave a more appropriate response.

"The training was a challenge, but it was also fun at times. I learned a lot and made several good friends. I'd like to go back someday to see more of San Antonio."

She seemed pleased with my answer. She told me that Sergeant Kennedy would have someone escort me to my barracks. I saluted again, did my best about face, and proceeded back to the sergeant's office.

Sergeant Kennedy had already summoned Airman Brown to accompany me to my new home. While we waited, she gave me a folder of papers that included my itinerary for the next two days. For the most part, I would be learning the base as I went through the lengthy processing procedure. Airman Brown would serve as my guide, and we would be doing a lot of walking.

Juanita Brown might have been the sister of Sergeant Imler, my basic training instructor, except that Juanita was black and had an attractive hairstyle. They had a similar build and tone of voice, though I couldn't be sure because Juanita didn't shout her words.

We left the office. As soon as we were out of hearing distance, Juanita started to talk. "I've been here a little over two months and I love it. There are a lot of good looking guys and plenty of fun stuff to do. I'm a medic but not much happens on the shift that I work. The day shift people give the shots. That's okay with me because I hate doing that anyway. Most of the time the only thing I do is clean up after the day shift. Now and then someone comes in with a simple injury or something like that. Otherwise, I'm free to read magazines as long as I remember to do the hourly walk around of the building."

Before I could make a comment she continued. "Everyone calls me Nita. I have a little thing that I do on the side."

Finally, I got a word in. "What kind of thing?" "Well, I press and curl hair in my room for some of the women as well as arch their eyebrows (which she did with a single-edged razor). "And," she added, looking at my clip-on earrings, "I also pierce ears."

"On Saturday mornings I set up shop outside the barracks. I put a chair outside and guys know that from nine to noon they can get a haircut from me cheaper than at the base barbershop."

In the barracks, music drifted from nearly every room. Nita explained that between 1500 and 1700 the women were free to do whatever they liked. From 1800 onward, the barracks would be quiet as people like her would be trying to get some sleep before leaving for their jobs around 2200.

When we reached my room I was happy to see that I would be sharing it with only one person. The narrow beds were separated by two reasonably-sized chests of drawers. There was a single desk and two tall metal storing cabinets used as closets. The showers were at one end of the hall on each floor. My room was on the first floor and, according to Nita, I was restricted to the bathroom facilities on that floor. She said she would be going to chow at 1700 and invited me to join her.

Airman Brown left me on my own, adding that my roommate would probably not be arriving until after 1800 as she worked days and usually went to dinner before coming home. That was the first time I had heard anyone use the word "home" when referring to a military barracks. I liked the sound of it coming from Nita and hoped that soon I too would think of it the same way.

When Nita returned I was still in my uniform. "Girl, you are still wearing those blues? I know you have something sharper than that."

I had begun unpacking but had not quite finished. Nita stepped over to my closet and pulled out a pair of tan bell-bottoms and suggested I find a cute top to wear with them. She talked while I did a quick change.

"Almost everybody rushes home to change into civvies once they are finished working. So don't be wearing that uniform when off duty unless you want to get the reputation for being a GI Junkie. The only government issue item you want to wear or carry at all times, is your military ID."

We entered the mess hall and Nita turned and waved to a guy sitting at a table with another man and two women. Before I could ask, Nita said, "That guy's name is Jerry. He is dating Julie, the girl who is sitting next to him. The other two are just friends. We all hang out together when we can. They have been here a lot longer than I have."

Without missing a word, Nita raised two fingers to let

her friend know that he should hold the last two seats for us. We got our food and joined the group who were already on dessert. Nita made the introductions and everyone welcomed me. They all knew Nita and began telling me about some of her talents.

Julie, Jerry's girlfriend, asked when I had arrived. "Just a few hours ago, and I really like it so far. I'm in the same barracks with Nita."

"Well, just get ready because you will soon know everyone on the base that's worth knowing. Nita hasn't been here long at all, but she has a reputation because of her great singing voice. She is in the chapel choir, and since she joined a lot more of us are getting up for service on Sunday mornings."

Wendy, who had been nodding her head in agreement, chimed in, "And on top of the singing, Nita is always the first to learn the newest dances way ahead of the rest of us."

At nineteen, I still had not gotten my ears pierced. The most fashionable earrings were for those who had earned their right to wear them by enduring the discomfort of having a needle (in this case a sewing needle) of some type passed through their earlobes. The number of shots I had taken in both arms did nothing to convince me that having someone push a needle through my earlobe was going to be fun. After going back and forth, first yes, then no,

I halfheartedly made a promise to Nita that on Saturday night I would allow her to do the procedure.

On that ominous evening, we started out by playing cards with a couple of other friends in Nita's room. She had a portable record player and a stack of LPs (long playing vinyl records). Her favorite group was Smoky Robinson and the Miracles, but she had all the soul singers. We sang along with our individual favorite artists while drinking rum and cokes and screwdrivers. Nita was the best singer and, when she sang The Temptations' *Just My Imagination*, everyone in the room stopped talking to listen. She closed her eyes and faded into a space that had nothing to do with the crowded room we were in.

Freda, the only smoker present, became so engrossed that she carelessly stubbed out her cigarette without even looking at it. Any other time, she was careful to save the butt to relight later on. But that night Freda had begun swaying to the music as she sipped her cocktail. A bit tipsy and distracted, she ground the cigarette into the ashtray before realizing what she had done.

"Damn it, Nita. Look what you made me do. I just wasted damn near half a cigarette listening to you." Everyone except Freda laughed.

When I appeared to be sufficiently drunk, Nita retrieved the piercing kit from her top drawer. The needle was already threaded. She had cut a small potato in half.

She placed the flat side of the potato firmly behind my ear lobe and picked up the needle. I suggested that maybe one more rum and coke was in order before we took the next step. I had already downed my limit of three but still felt uncertain and nervous.

Nita was just about out of patience with me and threatened that either she would pierce my ears right then or not at all. For the second time, she pressed the cool potato to the already numb sliver of flesh that was my ear. I had been squeezing an ice cube against it off and on through three Marvin Gaye songs.

I pulled the four crumpled one-dollar bills from my pocket, the fee for the service, and placed them in the center of the card table. With that, Nita raised the needle and, without wavering, passed it through my left earlobe. Before saying a word or giving me time to respond to what had just happened, she pierced the other one. When she had finished, a long piece of thread dangled from each ear. She snipped the thread and tied the ends together making a loop—my first pair of pierced earrings.

For the next week I would pull the thread back and forth in order to keep the tiny hole from closing. Barbara, one of the other women, told me to rub Vaseline on the tender lobes to keep them moist and to enable the thread to glide back and forth. Since she was the only woman I knew with two holes in each ear, I accepted her instruction without question. She reminded me that, if I decided to get extra piercings, wearing more than a single pair of earrings while in uniform was a dress code violation. She need not have told me that. While I had not felt any pain when Nita pushed the needle through, the anxiety leading up to that moment was not something I planned to go through again.

For phase two, Nita took a straw from the broom we used for sweeping the hallway and snapped it in half before burning it on both ends. I closed my eyes while she removed the threads and replaced them with the straws. A full month later, with shaky hands, I put in the shiny little balls I had been eager to wear.

It was just about that time that Margie Perkins stole the first boy I had ever dated, pigeon-toed Donald Johnson. Margie was not as good a dancer as Nita, but she seldom said no when asked. And so it happened that, when I saw Margie and Donald doing a slow grind to Marvin Gaye and Tammi Terrell's *Heaven Must Have Sent You From Above*, I knew it was over. Looking back, I know that was simply part of growing up. Still, men far outnumbered women on base, so it seemed to me that Margie could have left Donald to me.

A better friend was Rita Snowden, a beautiful young woman inside and out. We affectionately described her as being light, bright, and damned near white. Her blue green eyes sparkled when she laughed, and she was almost always laughing. Born and raised in Norfolk, Virginia, when she tired of hearing anyone mispronounce Norfolk, she would stop the perpetrator and make him or her repeat a short phrase. "Here's how you can remember the correct way to say Norfolk. Repeat after me: We don't smoke, we don't drink, norfuk, norfuk, norfuk."

CHAPTER 4

Charlie

I first met Staff Sergeant (four stripes) Charles Nolan Williams on a rainy afternoon in the Airmen's Club. He was in his second four-year stretch with three years to complete before getting out. Nita was trying to teach me to shoot pool, and he was making fun of my efforts but in such a way that I could not even pretend to be angry. Instead, I asked if he thought he could do any better. It was a thoughtless retort as most of the guys played pool on a regular basis. Nita and I had been surprised to find a table free rather than having to take a number and wait for one.

Though he had not picked me up at my barracks, that wound up being our first date. Most everyone called him Charlie. He was seven years older than I but he didn't look it. He already had a college degree when he enlisted. As a talented musician, he played piano, flute, and saxophone with equal ease. The tenor saxophone was his instrument of choice. When he squeezed his eyes shut and bent over while playing that horn, it was as if he forgot everything and everyone else. The man and the music became one. It was impossible to hear and watch him play without moving with the flow of those long, sustained notes.

Initially, I wished he were taller, but his charm, good looks, and great sense of humor more than compensated for the fact that I did not have to stand on tip-toe to kiss him.

I don't know why I ever thought that was romantic anyway. When anyone referred to his size, he would snap back with a smile, "I may be a small piece of leather, but I'm well put together." And so he was. He could have modeled briefs, swim trunks or anything else that exposed his legs and feet. As far as I was concerned, those were his best features.

Charlie believed that our bodies should be honored. For him that meant no smoking, regular exercise, sensible eating, and drinking in moderation. Part of his daily regimen included swallowing several vitamin supplements each morning after having run three miles.

He played tennis frequently and better than most other players on the base. A few people sought him for lessons and became proficient enough to enjoy the sport. I wanted to learn but only under certain conditions. Because I lacked basic coordination and confidence, if there were onlookers or others waiting to play when we arrived at the court, I would refuse to go on. After a few such antics, Charlie gave up trying to teach me. Though I never learned to play, I also did not tire of watching him stretch to the limit to deliver a perfect serve. Swimming did not come to him as easily, but that didn't lessen his enthusiasm. Instead, he somehow found extra time for practicing until he mastered the technique. I shunned his offer for lessons because I did not want to get my hair wet.

Charlie laughed at my reasoning and told me that I had a choice. "You know you could wear it in an Afro. Then getting it wet would not be an issue."

He had a point, but at that time in my life I thought I looked better with my hair straightened. Hair had always been a big deal to me and to many, if not most, black females. But in the late 60s, it became even more so as we black women debated within ourselves and with each other what it meant to be black and beautiful. I was torn between trying to be an Angela Davis or Diana Ross look alike.

During the short time that I dated Donald Johnson, we spent one night at a motel. The next morning he showered first because I wanted to take a bath and not be rushed. When I leaned in to turn on the water, it came flooding out of the shower-head rather than from the faucet where I held my hand waiting to test the temperature. I screamed while turning the controls off. But the damage had been done. My hair was soaked. By the time we got back to base, it had dried into a wild nest. Once in my room, I slipped a note under Nita's door asking if she would press my hair as soon as possible. Diana won that round.

When I did go the way of the Afro, I went all the way.

It was so huge that people wanted to touch it.

"Is it yours or is that a wig?" they asked.

"It's mine." I answered, smiling and feeling good about my looks. Shallow though it may have been, I had something that made people notice me, and I liked the feeling.

I remember the first time Charlie complimented me on my legs. Mini-skirts were in and, though I felt my legs were too skinny to wear them, Nita and a persuasive sales girl convinced me otherwise. We had driven the five miles from base to Tacoma Mall. Neither of us was looking for anything in particular. We merely wanted a change from shopping at the Base Exchange or the BX as we all called it. The BX was okay for most of our needs and the prices were unbeatable. But there was not much of a selection of the latest fashions.

The mall, on the other hand, had at least two dozen stores including our favorites, the 5-7-9 Shop, Jay Jacobs, and Lyons. The skirt had come off a sale rack at Jay Jacobs. Late one afternoon, not too long after I bought it, Charlie came by to pick me up for a movie. The theater was several blocks from my barracks and we had planned to drive. But when he saw me in the short skirt, he gave a long whistle and then a big smile. "Do you mind if we walk? I want the fellows to see me with this fine sistah."

I could not say anything in return. He clasped my hand and we set off not caring if we got to the show on time or not. Bliss is the word that describes what I felt at that moment. It was a new sensation.

That was one of his many strong suits. He knew how to make just about anyone feel better about themselves. Both his male friends and my girlfriends trusted him as a confidant. He outranked me and several others in our circle. More rank meant better pay, and Charlie never seemed to be broke. His buddies often sought him out when they were short of cash.

"Hey Man, let me hold a twenty until payday," one of them would say.

And he would hand it over without any follow-up comments. However, if the borrower did not pay him back, he need not ask for another favor involving money.

In retrospect, I should have thanked Margie Perkins for *stealing* Donald Johnson. Had she not, I might have missed the chance of having a down-to-earth man not only demonstrate his love for me but also model what it meant to be a true friend.

Soon after we met, Charlie began taking courses towards his master's degree at Pacific Lutheran University (PLU) in Tacoma. The government contracted civilian instructors to come onto base and teach evening classes. This was common practice at military facilities all over the country. Charlie encouraged the rest of us to at least take advantage of such programs if we were not inclined or able to pay for courses off base. A few followed his lead.

Leigh Aiken, one of eight women in my barracks who had a single room, would become a life-long friend. She claims that the first words out of my mouth when we met were, "When are you leaving so I can have your room?" She had already received her orders for Germany before I arrived.

Our memories differ on the timing of the room conversation. As I recall it, we had known each other at least a couple of days before I asked. I had no idea that regulations required that I complete a request form and submit it to the barracks commander, who would pass it on to our First Sergeant, who would then weigh the merits of my request compared to the request of others with more seniority. Instead, Leigh and I worked it out between the two of us. I moved in and the room was mine for the rest of my time at McChord.

My new room was located at the end of the long hallway, only a few feet from the exit. I knew that after dark Charlie could come and go without being observed by anyone else. There were three other rooms on that floor that offered the same advantage, and we all covered for each other as our boyfriends came and went.

On a rare sunny day in August of '69 I got the call to "come as soon as you can." Charlie drove me the forty miles from McChord to Sea-Tac, consoling me all the way. At that point Daddy was still alive, but he passed on while I was flying above the clouds on my way to him.

Daddy's high blood pressure was a chronic problem though he had never been overweight. If anything, he was too thin. Nevertheless, on a hot, humid morning in St. Louis, he collapsed on the upstairs landing just outside his bedroom and died eight hours later.

The fact that Otis Harris had not chosen to intervene nor even question the sick behavior demonstrated by his wife toward Sis and me had not weakened our love for him. Respect, though, has to be earned, and time ran out before he scaled that mountain. My sister and I are both in our sixties, yet even now, when we speak of our father, we remain unable to come to terms with his inability to protect us. His wife had the freedom to whip us at any time, even in his presence. Sometimes Beatrice struck our legs with a rolled newspaper or yardstick, but she preferred using a leather belt. At least once she beat Rosemarie with an extension cord. If Sis cried then, that would have been the only time that she gave Beatrice the satisfaction of seeing her tears. I, on the other hand, began bellowing and begging, often before my legs ever felt the sting from the belt.

The funeral service took place at Pilgrim Congregational Church even though Otis had never felt comfortable there. Beatrice had joined the prestigious church before marrying my father. Our blue-collar family had no place in it given that the other handful of blacks that attended were all professionals.

A gnat flew around my father's face. I wanted to reach out and slap it between my palms. Daddy lay very still even when it entered one of his nostrils. I watched intently for the next several minutes for the insect to come out again. It did not. Surely that was proof that Daddy was really dead. Otherwise, even shallow breathing would have sent the gnat back out into view.

My anxiety that a loved one or I might be buried alive seems to have come from nowhere. There had been no nightmare or event that precipitated my strange fixation. But still the fear was real. Maybe it had to do with Grandma Ellen's wake. I was almost six when she died. The wake took place in the front room of her house. She was seventy-five and had buried her husband and two of her eleven children. I remember wondering when it was that she would finally wake up. I did not want her to go.

We were all there waiting for something miraculous to happen, or at least I thought that was the reason everyone had come. The tiny house shrank even more as friends waded in throughout the evening. The heavy fragrance of fresh flowers, combined with the sweet waters and colognes that women had dabbed generously behind their ears and on their necks, made breathing difficult.

Everyone spoke in soft voices; some even whispered.

Such behavior seemed counterproductive if in fact the "wake" was to be successful. Grandma Ellen's small body did not touch either side of the simple wooden box that would be lowered into the ground the next morning.

Someone had draped a sheer white netting over part of the box, preventing us from seeing her face clearly. The reason for the veil, an aunt told me, was to keep the mosquitoes from bothering her.

Why, I wondered—but didn't ask—were the adults taking so many measures to prevent her waking up?

There had been no waking time for Daddy, who was Grandma Ellen's sixth born. I had witnessed that gnat disappear inside his nostril and watched attentively for it to emerge. A sense of relief brushed over me as his face disappeared when the undertaker lowered the polished wooden lid. In the end, just like his mother, Daddy was placed in the ground but in a nicer box called a coffin.

I returned to Washington and re-entered my routine with no outward show of grief. Charlie remained attentive as always and, as an added act of caring, allowed me to drive his car more frequently than before. Ignoring the taunts of his buddies, he had taught me to drive the dark blue, four-speed Corvair soon after we started dating. The guys he hung out with teased him right in front of me.

"Man, she gon' ruin your transmission. She will never learn to drive a stick, especially not with all the hills around here. You better make sure you keep her out in an open flat field."

Once, his best buddy Marvin asked, "You got your insurance paid up?" Charlie, ignoring the implication, made a reply about his no-fault policy, to which Marvin said, "Naw, man. I'm not talkin' about your car insurance. I'm talking about your life insurance. You got that paid up? Because if you don't, you may want to take care of that. It would be a shame to see your mother not get the payoff once you been killed in a car wreck."

But Charlie was not put off in the least. Once I got the hang of driving that car without a lot of false starts, I thought I was hot stuff. Even Marvin had to admit that I had quickly learned to shift the gears without stripping them. So when he called Charlie and asked for a ride to his part-time job off base, and I showed up alone to pick him up, there was no way for him to get out of putting his rear end in the passenger seat and not giving me any lip. I took the longest route possible to our destination.

In February of 1970, a year before my tour of duty was due to end, I received orders that I was being sent overseas the next month. Always the optimist, my boyfriend tried to help me see the positive. Most overseas assignments were a minimum of eighteen months, he reminded me. "You are lucky. You only have eleven months left. I'll write to you every week, and in no time we will be together again."

We promised each other that once I returned we would never again be separated, and Nita vowed to keep an eye on him in my absence.

The Air Force band is a unique unit within that branch

of service. It was made up primarily of men. Being a member only added to Charlie's popularity with the women. He played more than one instrument and wrote most of the music for the jazz band he performed in on weekends. His prowess on the tennis court was another hot topic, and WAFs, even those who had no interest in the game, gathered around the court just to spy on him in his tight shorts. I tried to take comfort in the knowledge that Nita had my best interest at heart. Still, I prayed that he would propose to me before I left the States, but he did not.

The base in Turkey was considerably smaller than the previous two where I had been stationed. The spring climate was much kinder than what I had left behind. In place of days on end of rain and overcast skies, I breathed in the cool, dry air of a land that boasted great bodies of water, hills, mountains, and seemingly endless fields where various crops thrived.

Established in the late 50s, Karamursel Air Force Base served as a listening post to intercept Russian radio transmissions. I was there when the first commercial airliner was hijacked and can remember clearly all personnel being restricted to base for several days after the incident. Such restraints made no sense, as we were thousands of miles away.

For the most part I never experienced having to adjust to Turkish society and was grateful for the option of remaining secluded on base with other Americans. After all, at twenty-one, having never before traveled outside the United States, the idea of being so close to Russia was more than a little unnerving.

Nikita Khruschev was no longer in power, but I remembered being terrified a few years earlier when, as leader of the USSR (Union of Soviet Socialist Republic), he instigated the Cuban missile crisis. It was in the fall of 1962. I was a sophomore in high school and was convinced that I would not live to graduate, as the world would be destroyed way before then. The Cuban missile crisis was the closest we came to nuclear war. With the approval of Fidel Castro, Khrushchev had assembled satellite missiles on the island of Cuba. President John F. Kennedy did not back down and issued an ultimatum that resulted in Khrushchev dismantling the missiles and returning them to Russia.

Still, my memory of his violent outbursts at the United Nations caused me to wonder about his successor being of like mind. What if a similar catastrophe occurred while I was so far from the people I loved and who loved me? How likely was it that Turkey might be targeted or, worse still, attacked?

In my mind, Karamursel was scary for a lot of reasons, but Master Sergeant Eleanor Rigsby was not one of them. She was my First Sergeant, but her easy smile and friendly manner pegged her as a cream puff compared to my basic training sergeant. Eleanor stood six feet tall. The contrast between her smooth pecan-colored skin and green eyes made it next to impossible not to stare. Everyone must have commented on her beautiful eyes when first meeting her, just as I did. Uncomfortable with the compliment, she smiled impishly and dropped her head. "Finally," I thought, "here is a real person who is not hung up on the fact that she outranks me."

Eleanor was the name I gave her because it fit. In my opinion, her birth name, Emma Jean, was too harsh and country sounding for the elegant woman she was. She had gone by Jean all her adult life. That was okay, but still not quite right. It didn't take long before I had the other WAFs calling her Eleanor, in private of course. When in uniform and conducting military business, she was Sergeant or First Sergeant Rigsby to all of us. She was the first black woman I'd met who not only owned a set of golf clubs but also knew how to use them. That fascinated me because in 1970 it was even more unusual to see a black golfer than a black tennis player.

I accompanied her to the on-base clubhouse several times. One of the written rules that dictated women's daily lives was that we were not allowed on the course until 1300 hours, one o'clock in the afternoon. Of course, by that time it was generally too hot for anyone to play. Eleanor would show up at 0700 when the place opened and demand entry.

Perhaps the Air Force men who made the rules had

taken their cue from the manner in which Turkish men treated their women. But such would not be the case on the base; not if Eleanor Rigsby had any say in it. By the time I met her, she had already been using the driving range routinely on a weekly basis, though she said at first the opposition she faced was intimidating. Nevertheless, she had persisted in getting the signs removed that stated the unfair policy and bringing with her other WAFs who played. Two of them became regulars on the course but, unlike Eleanor, they were both white. I never swung a club but I enjoyed the company of all three women as much as I liked being viewed as a member of the resistance.

RHIP—Rank Has Its Privileges—was a slogan commonly used in the Air Force, usually by those of us with low rank and few privileges. Because Eleanor was a Master Sergeant, the Air Force had shipped her car to Turkey. The 1970 two-toned blue Dodge Challenger would be the second stick shift automobile I would drive—but not often and never off base.

In our orientation briefing, we were reminded that we had landed in a Muslim country where people trusted that Allah protected at all times those who believed. Even if they dared passing at high speeds on an uneven two-lane road, their lives would be spared—unless, of course, it was their time to depart this world for the next. We would be taking our lives into our own hands if we drove off base.

First Sergeant Rigsby maintained that the warnings about Turkish drivers were exaggerated. On more than one occasion, I squeezed my eyes shut as she entered a curve on the wrong side of the road having just passed a vehicle that, according to Eleanor, was not roadworthy in the first place.

There I was, thousands of miles from home, surrounded by people whose customs and culture were as different as black from white to my own, yet I lacked the curiosity to take advantage of a once in a lifetime opportunity. I just wanted that year to be over. Nevertheless, on our drives to shop in Yalova and other nearby towns, the sights and sounds of that far away land captivated me.

One of the familiar images still fixed in my mind is that of women working in the fields. They planted and gathered fruits and vegetables wearing the traditional Turkish dress. Not all women wore headscarves, but those who did chose bright, colorful, patterned designs. The bent over women looked like oversized wild flowers. Their attire contrasted with the drab work clothes I had worn as a sharecropper.

When I was growing up my Aunt Frances had a fig tree in her backyard. I had tried them but they were not among my favorite fruits. The figs in Turkey became my fruit of choice. I'm not certain whether they tasted any different from those grown on a tree in Tennessee or if I was becoming a bit more open in my attitude about trying new things.

Eleanor would insist that I "taste it before you decide you don't like it." She was right about the figs, but the coffee remained bitter, no matter how much sugar I added. After two or three attempts, she gave up trying to get me to like Turkish coffee.

The eleven months passed quickly. Charlie and I had kept our promise of writing often to one another. About two months before my return to the States, he proposed to me in a letter. This move may have been prompted in part by the fact that I had told him that I was dating. Nita had written to tell me about a conniving woman named Karen Jackson. Neither of us had liked her from the get-go. She wore a wig—a blonde one. And though she would have been welcomed to hang out with us in Nita's make-do beauty salon, she always had an excuse for not doing so. Maybe she thought we would strip her of her store-bought hair.

In any event, when I found out that she was after my guy, I imagined yanking the thing off her head in public and chasing her down.

Nita shared my feelings. In one of her letters, she wrote to me, "Mary," as I was called back then, "you should see how blatant she is in flirting with Charlie. She is always in his face swinging that phony blonde hair all over the place. I feel like snatching it off her head and slapping the shit out of her with it."

Naturally, when I asked Charlie about Karen in one of my letters, he wrote back explaining that he was not interested in "that woman" but did not want to hurt her feelings. They were seeing each other but only casually. "Yeah, right," I thought. In any event, once I had his written proposal, I knew that he was serious. While he may have been interested in Karen, it was me he had asked to be his wife. I floated on a cloud for days. I thought I should make him wait for an answer, but that notion lasted about three minutes. The next day, I mailed my letter saying yes.

Although I had high expectations for what awaited me back in the beautiful state of Washington, leaving Turkey was still bittersweet. Eleanor had become more like a big sister than my boss, and I would miss her. At the same time, I looked forward to the long flight back to the States. My first flight ever had been from San Antonio to Seattle, Washington, in 1967. Even then, I hoped that someday I would be an airline hostess. Once I was back home, I would be one step closer to fulfilling that dream. I made my rounds saying goodbye to friends. The few tears that might have come were halted as I replayed the memory of my second flight, the one that had brought me from New York to Istanbul almost a year earlier.

The Boeing 747 was more than six times the size of our house in Eads. How in the world, I had wondered, would it ever leave the ground? To my amazement, that's exactly what happened and I was instantly hooked on flying. Then and now I have a fear of heights in tall buildings. I cannot, for instance, stand or sit on the balcony of a hotel room that's above the third floor. But somehow being six miles above the earth in an aluminum and steel tube skimming the clouds at five hundred miles an hour doesn't bother me one bit. More than that, the idea causes my heart to race with anticipation. This phenomenon defies reason but is my reality.

As I stood next to Eleanor wanting to stay and to go at the same time, I needed only recall the thrill I knew would come when the aircraft sped down the runway taking me with it and making me part of the endless sky.

Two days later, in February of 1971, at McGuire Air Force Base in New Jersey, I received my honorable discharge and returned to Tacoma, Washington, as a civilian. As I made my way along the concourse at Sea-Tac, I did miss the tingle I had felt in times past when onlookers smiled and even pointed toward the tall black girl who proudly wore the U.S. Air Force Blue.

CHAPTER 5

Settling In

Master Sergeant Johnny Hudson lived off base with his wife Sadye and three kids. But in 1971, Johnny was in Viet Nam. Before he got shipped out, the Hudsons routinely welcomed Charlie and me into their home. Sadye continued to invite us even in her husband's absence.

Sadye was a five-foot-two, dark skinned, Rubenesque figure with a smile that covered her entire face. Her energy came in spurts and when she was feeling well, she could do ten things at once. But when she had a headache or an upset stomach or the blues, she would quite simply shut down and no amount of prodding would serve to get her up again until she was ready.

Years later I found the following note she had written me: "Dear Mary, unless hell freezes over, don't disturb me. Rant and rave, but I forgot the records and left them at Liz's. Remind me to get a gift for the kids to take to the birthday party anytime after 1000 hours. Thanks, Sadye".

The note was typical of how she operated all during our friendship. Having put me on notice, she could then crawl back into bed and be assured that when she got up hours later, I would very likely have collected the records from Liz and purchased a gift for the kids to take to the birthday party they were attending. I loved her primarily because, most of the time, she was vibrant and threw off energetic sparks that could charge a whole room, and she had a heart of gold.

There was always something going on at Johnny and Sadye's place, especially on weekends. We had amazing cookouts on their huge homemade backyard grill. Nearby neighbors would drop by sometimes, pretending to need to borrow some tool or other. Three hours later they would be among the boisterous volleyball and Bid Whist participants. Music played a key role in every event they hosted. Johnny was naturally charming and loved to dance, sing, and generally clown around. We were all drawn to him as if he were a life-sized, dark chocolate magnet.

Johnny was no more than twelve years older than I, but in common with two other young women who preceded me down the aisle on his arm, he was my first choice as surrogate dad. Since he was half way around the world, I needed to find a substitute.

After the Hudsons', the Walker residence was the second most popular off-base home away from home. Staff Sergeant Jimmy Walker had *re-upped* and lived off base with his wife Liz, their two daughters, and a Great Dane that used to scare me senseless. Jimmy had the physique of a body builder, though it was his winning personality and ability to calm even the most nervous bride that made him the perfect choice to walk me down the aisle. His wife Liz made me a simple, long, white gown.

Charlie still had two months to go before completing eight years of military service. His active duty status meant that we could use the base chapel for our wedding.

On the last day of October 1971, Charlie and I stood at the front of the church with all our friends filling the pews. "I, Mary Alice Harris, take you, Charles Nolan Williams, to be my husband." The ceremony was simple. None of my relatives were present. They were thousands of miles away. Charlie's sister, Joan, had recently moved to the area from their home in North Carolina and was able to join in the celebration. Charlie took me home to meet his parents and other family members, but not until my last name was the same as his. Mr. and Mrs. Williams still lived in the house my new husband had grown up in. They welcomed me as if I had been part of the family all my life.

Soon after his honorable discharge, Charlie began looking for teaching jobs. He sent his resumé to various elementary and high schools in several states. It did not take long before Pierce County Schools in Tacoma offered him a job as band teacher at five local elementary schools.

We lived in a nice second floor walk-up apartment located near a bus line. I walked two blocks, caught the number 7, and arrived at my part-time job in the mall fifteen minutes later. Charlie traveled from school to school, so he drove our one car, the same one he had taught me to drive.

Charlie was working toward his master's degree, playing in a jazz band, and teaching tennis and piano to three students in addition to his regular teaching job. It sounds like a lot for one man, but he was not yet thirty. We were young, healthy, and in love. Everyone who knew us thought the romance would last forever.

Our years together were full. We enjoyed hanging out with our friends and going to movies, especially drive-ins. Charlie had access to the piano in one of the music rooms at the university. "Hi, Baby," he would say over the phone. "Do you want to go with me over to the campus later on?"

I knew what that meant. If it were a nice day, we would stroll the grounds before entering the building. But if it was raining, we parked as close as possible and ran to the entrance. Charlie would sit at the piano and play chords over and over, intermittently transposing the notes to blank music sheets spread around him. I watched quietly and listened as he took what was in his head and transformed it into something I could hear and feel. What he gave—what we shared—would have been more than enough for most women. And it should have been enough for me.

All I could dream about was working for an airline. But Charlie said, as he always did, "In the meantime, why not take some classes at TCC?" Tacoma Community College was an easy walk from our home. I enrolled in a two-year business administration program. Taking classes and working in the record department at JC Penney's filled the days and weeks following my wedding. But I just wanted to fly.

I targeted Eastern Airlines as my next employer. After three interviews and the same number of rejection letters, I decided to try a new approach. There are several passages in the book of Proverbs that advise men to give in to a woman's request lest they be worn out from her nagging. The plan seemed worth trying regardless of the gender of the HR person at the airlines. I became a familiar face at all of the larger airlines' employment offices. It was easy as most were housed within Sea-Tac Airport or nearby.

The first time I sat down across the desk from the man who had the power to grant my wish, he told me quite succinctly, "Come back next week wearing a skirt. I need to see your legs." I hadn't the sense or the nerve to be offended. Today, I'd be filing a lawsuit. But the year was 1972. I returned to his office a week later wearing a fitted skirt that stopped three inches above my knees. I had been filling out applications and going for five-minute compulsory interviews for a year. In the end it was my short skirt that landed me the job of a lifetime.

Though we had been married only a year, Charlie was not only supportive but seemed genuinely happy about the outcome. He understood that, for me, it was a dream come true. Neither of us knew it then, but this great turn of events marked the beginning of our final chapter as husband and wife.

CHAPTER 6

Up, Up and Away

When I left Tacoma bound for United's training center in Chicago, I had no background information to help me see what lay ahead. The only thing that mattered was I had been selected, skinny legs and all. The competition had been intense and the training was said to be rigorous. Initially I did not feel intimidated. Every hurdle I had cleared, especially basic military training, should put me in good stead to weather anything United Airlines might throw at me. I was focused and had but one goal, to return home in six weeks proudly wearing the wings that identified me as one of a unique group. The industry had been changing during the process of my multiple interviews. In 1970 some of the carriers began hiring men, making "airline hostess" an obsolete term. I would be a stewardess and my male counterparts, stewards.

Goodbyes are never easy. On our last evening together I cried. How could I be happy and miserable at the same time? I had not calculated the cost and now wanted to find a way of bargaining for a better deal. I loved my husband and hated the thought of the upcoming separation, but there was no escaping the mandatory training. We both knew I had to do it. I never considered turning down the offer and, if such a thought entered Charlie's mind, he kept it there.

"Whatever it takes, we will do this together. We will figure it out as we go along. I love you, baby, and you are going to breeze through that training the same way you have done everything else you've put your mind to. When the training is over, we will have the rest of our lives together."

I fell asleep in his arms holding on to every word he had said.

The next afternoon when I arrived at the designated meeting place at Chicago's O'Hare Airport, I was tingling with excitement. The arrangement to get from the airport to the training center was not unlike my experience when I reported for basic training in the Air Force. The instructions in the letter were very specific and included a map that pinpointed the pickup location and departure times and gave a detailed description of the bus.

The first girl I saw was Debbie Voelker, 5'7" and statuesque with pencil straight blonde hair. She could have been a Playboy Bunny. But the first thing I noticed was her captivating smile; her teeth actually sparkled.

"I'll bet nobody told her to come back wearing a skirt," I thought as she walked straight over to me. Her easy way of talking made me feel relaxed and happy. Before we ever spotted the bus, we had agreed to ask if we could be roommates. We knew from the informational packet that there were no single rooms.

Kimberlee Blake strode toward us wearing a big grin. I liked her immediately. Even in flats she was easily six feet tall, but that day she wore a pair of chocolate three-inch heeled leather boots. She was even more stunning than Voelker, primarily due to her height, thin frame and thick, curly hair. Here again was a woman that no interviewer would have turned down. She had a wicked sense of humor matched with a distinctive voice that always seemed on the verge of laughter. Kimberlee was a native of Seattle; we had actually been on the same flight but hadn't known it.

The next two to join us were Cher Powell and Conchetta Richio. Conchetta had more luggage than any two of us and looked like a life-sized doll. The opposite of Kimberlee, Conchetta just made the five foot two minimum height requirement. By the time the bus pulled up, we were all chattering with such excitement that we might have missed it except for the nice driver who stepped onto the curb and called out to us. That was the beginning of our journey into a whole new world.

The training center looked to us something like a

prison camp. There was a guard at the gate, and a ten-foot fence of wire mesh enclosed the entire complex. The main building had served as a bomb shelter during World War II. As best we could tell, not much renovation had been done since to improve its cellblock appearance.

Almost as soon as we met her, most of us began calling Debbie Voelker by her last name. *Debbie* just didn't seem to fit. Voelker, Conchetta and I shared a room designed for four people. Our small class of twenty-one women and two men gave us an advantage. Conchetta needed every bit of the extra closet space that a fourth person would have used. Our bathroom had a single shower stall but enough counter area that two of us could put on our makeup at the same time. I don't think anyone slept that first night. Nevertheless, the following morning we arrived in the Assembly Room ten minutes earlier than scheduled for orientation. We spent the whole of that day listening to the four stewardesses who would be conducting most of our training. To us, they were sky goddesses.

If anyone had come with the idea that learning to be a steward or stewardess was nothing more than putting on a tailored uniform and serving food and drinks miles above the earth, their notions were dispelled before we ever got our first coffee break. We were introduced to the history of United Airlines through film clips, lectures, and a series of newspaper clippings arranged in scrapbooks bearing the company logo. We were given an overview of company policy, federal air regulations, airline codes, and fleet recognition. We learned basic definitions and how to identify—among other things—flaps, ailerons, stabilizers, and rudders.

I could hardly wait for the chance to see my next airplane close up. Early on, and until they retired it from the fleet, the Super DC-8, or Stretch 8 as we called it, was my favorite airplane to watch on takeoff. In my estimation, not even the Concorde's configuration compared to the simple, long, sleek, elegant lines of the Stretch 8. I pulled off the road countless times as I approached O'Hare Airport to see if I could spot one headed to the runway. When I did, my eyes stayed on it until the tail of that beautiful bird disappeared into the clouds.

At the end of our first day, the instructors saddled us down with pounds of written material to be used in the classes required for graduation. Still, our enthusiasm did not wane. Well, at least not immediately.

Personal grooming, hair and makeup classes were part of the curriculum. I had worn makeup but no one had ever showed me how to apply it. Our instructors encouraged us to wear false lashes if our own were thin or short. Once, before I got the hang of it, I glued them on backwards. I knew they felt odd but did not know why until I boarded a flight and another stewardess told me what I had done.

Though we needed a passing grade in all our classes,

the week spent in emergency training was the one we most dreaded. It loomed as the final obstacle between walking to the podium to receive the coveted wings or being spirited away in the night and sent home. Everything led up to it, and our anxiety level was off the charts by the time we met that specialized group of instructors. All of them were male.

We climbed up inflated slides after having jumped into them to escape simulated burning aircraft. We crawled into authentic life rafts for the purpose of locating and identifying the survival equipment they held. We yanked open doors and windows on airplane mockups until the muscles in our arms and backs screamed. A long soak was what we all wanted, but there were no bathtubs. Instead we would stand in the shower for at least ten minutes trying to relieve the soreness. We all rooted for each other and worked as a team to succeed. At the end of five weeks, we had lost two members—one of them the only other black woman who had started out with us. Voelker and I were the only two who were married. Our husbands came to the graduation ceremony and pinned on our wings.

After graduation United paid for our rooms at an airport hotel for one week. We were then expected to secure permanent lodging. Voelker and I spotted an announcement on the United bulletin board. The Carousel Apartments, located in Schiller Park just three miles from O'Hare, was nicknamed the Stew Zoo. There was even a shuttle bus to take us back and forth. Our roommates, Shirley Moore and Tresa Anderson, flew for the now defunct Ozark Airlines.

I was the oldest of all the women in that apartment but, in some ways, the least mature. With the exception of the love of family members, the first eighteen years of my life had not been much fun. I viewed those years in the early 70s as my opportunity to make up for lost experiences.

Deciding to legally change my name during that time, was little more than an outward statement of self expression. Mary Alice was the name my parents had given me after my maternal grandmother. However, in the small southern town where I grew up, almost no one pronounced it correctly. Mary Alice became Maeralice; by the time I reached adolescence, I hated the sound of it.

By 1974, my grandmother and my parents were long since dead. Nimbilasha suited me. It sounded exotic and sophisticated. Of course, it was immediately shortened to Nimbi by my family and friends. More than forty years later, when I return to the place where I grew up, to the few of my parent's friends still living, I am, and will forever be, Maeralice.

While changing my name was not one of them, I made plenty of mistakes, sometimes inflicting pain on people who didn't deserve it. But there came a moment when I realized that there are few, if any, do-overs in life. Time gone by is just that. On the plus side of things, my relationship with those women became the foundation on which I built friendships—indeed a sisterhood—that has lasted to this day.

A few weeks after we moved in, a beautiful girl from San Francisco, Wendy Guentner, joined us, bringing our number to six in a two-bedroom one-bath apartment. Wendy, with her husband's blessings, completed United's training several weeks after me. The three of us who were married did not appreciate the difficulties involved in preserving a long distance relationship. We would soon learn.

I remember once trying to get home to see Charlie. After six hours at O'Hare, three flights had left without me. Flying 'Space Available' is tricky in the best of situations. With no seniority, it was a nightmare. When I did get a seat on the last flight that day, I immediately fell sound asleep. When we touched down at Sea-Tac, I realized that Charlie and I would get to our apartment around 11 o'clock in the evening. Twenty- four hours later I would be on my way back to the same airport hoping to catch a return flight to Chicago. I decided to make the most of whatever time we had.

Once the plane was parked at the gate and the seat belt sign turned off, I retrieved my uniform coat from the overhead bin, slipped into the restroom and stripped. I stuffed my entire outfit into the already full tote bag and put on the coat. I buttoned it carefully and tied the belt securely around my waist.

Having now written these words, I wonder if I know the person I've just described. Charlie was thrilled and we toyed with the idea of getting a room at an airport hotel instead of making the drive to Tacoma. We should have. And I should have improvised more little romantic surprises instead of ultimately walking away from an incredibly wonderful man who loved me down to my toes.

I never asked him to relocate to Chicago, for that would have put him in a dilemma that he did not deserve. The teaching job he had taken at the five elementary schools came with a contract. I would not ask him to break it. After two years of infrequent trips home, my decision to call it quits was purely selfish and immature. My husband pleaded with me to "just hang in there with me a while longer."

Like a spoiled child, I wanted it all—my life as a stewardess and the ability to be with Charlie at the end of each trip. There was no way of having both. The choice I made way back then still haunts me at times. Charlie loved me, but he had his pride. When he accepted the fact that my mind was made up, he said yes to my request for a divorce. Going through with it stands out as my greatest personal failure.

Many years after we divorced I received an unexpected package in the mail from him. He had remarried and was clearing house. The large manila envelope contained a scrapbook that I don't even remember having. Inside were photographs, cards, letters and notes dating from 1969 to

1972. I studied our youthful faces with genuine grins as we looked into each other's eyes.

"Damn it." I thought again. "What was I using for brains when I left him?"

"Oh Charlie, I am so sorry," I said while pressing a favorite picture to my chest.

CHAPTER 7

Early Departure

Wendy got her transfer and moved home to San Francisco, and Voelker transferred to Denver. Three single women moved in. Lynda Warren, Debbie Johnson, and Sylvia Mischal were all new stewardesses. United hired them several months after I began flying. In the early 70s, airlines enforced weight restrictions. Luckily for me, at five feet nine inches and a hundred and twenty three pounds, I needed only weigh in twice a year to meet company requirements.

Lynda, Tresa, and Shirley loved to cook, and they were good at it. Eating was, and still is, in the top three of my ten most favorite things. We were perfectly matched. Lynda proved to be the best cook of all. She could create a small feast out of a sometimes-limited supply of ingredients available in our fridge and cupboards. It was not uncommon to find her making stacks of waffles from scratch in the middle of the night after one or two of us had come in hungry. It didn't matter if the late night arrival came in after a night at our favorite disco or at the end of an ugly three-day trip. The rattle of pots and pans summoned everyone to the kitchen. In no time we would all be gathered around the table laughing and talking as if it were the middle of the afternoon.

Shirley Moore, one of the two women who flew for Ozark, was a natural entertainer. She used to drape herself in shawls and scarves, singing and dancing around the apartment as she prepared to go out for the evening. Doctors had told her she would not live to be thirty. Shirley's response was, "They can kiss my ass."

She outmaneuvered death ten years longer than the doctors had predicted before Sickle Cell Anemia took her.

CHAPTER 8

A Man for All Seasons

I met the man who would become my second husband while he was married to my younger sister. At the time not one of us could have guessed where and how our paths were destined to join together. Ours is not a revisit to Peyton Place. There were no stolen glances across crowded rooms, no secret phone calls or subversive plots motivated by sensual desire. Any of these would be more believable than the truth, which is this:

After marrying Milton Odom, my oldest sister, Lorraine moved to South Bend, Indiana, in 1963; five years later my younger sister Rosemarie joined her. Sis (as I call her) and I had grown up together after being separated from Lorraine and our four brothers, all older than we. From our days in elementary school Sis, though younger, had assumed the role that should have been mine. She, more than I, behaved like the older sister, and that was fine by me. She tried desperately to teach me all the games that she learned from our brother Ed Roy when he came to visit. I was never any good at climbing trees or at shooting marbles or a BB gun. But my inability to catch on never discouraged her from trying.

When I joined the Air Force and left St. Louis, Rosemarie had one year of high school remaining. We had returned there as young teens after living with our grandparents in Tennessee for twelve years. Unlike our Tennessee experience, home life in St. Louis had been hell due to a tormented stepmother and a father who stood by and did nothing. Sis was smart and beautiful, and she wasn't afraid of anything. Adventurous by nature, she thought a new city—a new way of life—might be just the right ticket. South Bend was a natural choice given that Lorraine had lived there several years and seemed to like it.

Sis was always one to fight for justice. It was natural for her to get involved in the civil rights activities sponsored by the local NAACP. At one of these, she met James Cushing, an associate professor of physics at Notre Dame. Jim hated injustice as much as she did. Standing together in the face of a common adversary—in this case, segregation—can be a powerful magnet for pulling persons together who might not have met otherwise.

That a sister or brother of mine would marry outside our race seemed at once incredible and, at that time in this nation's history, dangerous. Never one to back down, my sister did the unthinkable. She married a white man. Our brothers, two of whom dated white women, were beside themselves. How could she? What was she thinking?

Lorraine and I were surprised and disappointed. The marriage came at a time when our culture was going all out to convince the rest of the country and ourselves that we were black and proud. Sis, I thought, would be denied by one race and shunned by the other. In spite of my fears for her, I did not run to her side as she had done for me all our lives.

For almost six years Rosemarie and Jim found that, within a certain cluster of university friends, life for them and their two daughters could be reasonably satisfying. There were challenges and hardships. Many of them had nothing to do with their being an inter-racial couple, though there was surely some of that too. When the divorce papers were signed, my sister had agreed that their children would be better off remaining in the home with their father. This situation at that time was rare in society. Children should always stay with the mother—or so went the reasoning of many.

Without any formal discussion, some of my family took sides. Once we had gotten to know Jim for the fine man that he was, our misplaced sense of outrage disappeared. Now, instead of asking "How could she marry a white man?" our cry became "How could she leave such a nice guy?"

Five years later Sis and Jim had both remarried, this time to people of their respective race. Lorraine had been diagnosed with breast cancer, and I was living the life of a single but somewhat wiser flight attendant. Gregg, the oldest of the Odom children, had gone off to college.

Lorraine and her husband Milton lived with their other three children "in the country," as they called it. They enjoyed gardening and always had plenty of fresh produce in season for their family and many friends. Jim had become one such friend when he was part of the family. That relationship endured long after he and Rosemarie divorced.

During the final two years of Lorraine's life, Jim more than once accompanied her and Milton to a Chicago hospital for cancer treatments. "It's always good to have a third person along," he said, "in the event of car trouble." Lorraine and Milton were grateful for his extraordinary kindness. Neither of them were scholars—far from it—but that didn't matter to Jim.

On occasion when I visited Lorraine, she would give me two bags of tomatoes or green beans that Milton and the kids had gathered from their garden. I was to keep one and, of the other, she would say, "Would you mind dropping this one off to Jim on your way out of town?" The last time she made such a request was in July of '79. She was very sick and in five months would be dead.

I remember placing the bag of vegetables on the floor of the car at my feet. I was with my friend Barbara, and I wished that my big sister had not given us the goodwill errand. Saying good-bye to her left me in a state of sadness; I did not feel like smiling or making small talk even with someone who had shown my sister such kindness. Our instructions were to leave the package at the back door if no one was home.

When we pulled up next to his garage, I had to catch my breath. There was Jim kneeling on the steep, slanted roof of his house tethered by a rope to the chimney. It wasn't clear whether he had heard our approach. We stood near the gate but dared not open it for fear the sound might startle him. After a minute or so, he turned toward us and raised a hand. "Hello," he said, as naturally as if he were standing on level ground right next to us.

I offered a halting apology and held up the brown paper sack. "Lorraine wanted us to drop off these vegetables for you and the girls. I'll just leave them by the back door unless you want me to take them inside."

"Give me a minute and I'll be right down."

"Please don't. We are headed back to Chicago and don't have much time. It seems an awful bother to…"

He had already placed one foot on the second rung of the long ladder before I could finish my sentence. When he reached the ground, he walked over to greet us and I introduced him to Barbara. He invited us in. Since he had gone to the trouble of removing the rope from around his waist and coming down to greet us, we followed him into the cool, bright kitchen.

"Where are the girls?" I asked. "It would be nice to see them."

"They're at a friend's. It's easier for me to do this kind of work if they are not around."

"Are you replacing the roof without help?"

"Yes, I am. I'm going on sabbatical for fall semester, and the money I would spend on hiring roofers can be put to better use taking the girls abroad."

Lorraine had once told me, "He is a better mother than many women that I know." Over time I saw that she was right. I had never seen my nieces when they were not well groomed, and they were always polite. The kitchen was clean and in order. I imagined the rest of the house to be the same.

Barbara and I declined his offer for something cold to drink and said we needed to be on our way. He thanked us for dropping off the package.

"Tell the girls I'm sorry to have missed them."

Up to that summer of '79, Jim and I had not seen each other on our own. Lorraine loved the girls, and their father made sure that she got to see them somewhat regularly.

Lorraine's youngest daughter was two months older than Jim and Rosemarie's oldest. Both my sisters had been pregnant at the same time.

The three of us stepped out the back door in a happy mood. Jim walked us to the car and opened both our doors before wishing us safe travel. Barbara commented on how nice it felt to meet such a gentleman.

We drove for a while in silence before I asked her what she thought of Lorraine's appearance. She had been with me on the previous visit which was her first time meeting my sister.

"Well, you can see that she is really sick, but she tries hard to keep going. Your sister is a determined woman, and you have told me how strong her faith is. Anything is possible, Nimbi. You mustn't give up hope."

I made two more trips back to see my sister before she died in January of 1980. Her husband and four children were devastated. One of the three children at home was in high school, and two in middle. Gregg had finished college and was married and working in St. Louis. In the aftermath of her death, I struggled with figuring out what my immediate response should be.

Even before our mother's death, Lorraine had always helped care for her six siblings. When Mama was gone, she stepped fully into that role. Now, it was my turn to try and pay back some of what she had given to me. I would soon learn that I didn't know how to do what she had done.

My knee jerk reaction was to get back to Indiana as soon as possible. At the time of her death, I had been living in a suburb of Washington D.C. United Airlines granted my request and transferred me to Chicago, a short drive from both my sisters' children.

I put my furniture in storage and moved in with Barbara, buying time to figure out what my next step should be. In the meantime, I made trips to South Bend, but my time with Lorraine's children was awkward. They hadn't expressed any desire or need for me to do anything. How could they? The person they most loved and who most loved them was gone, and that void could not be filled by anyone. My intentions were good but were fueled by misguided notions and feelings of obligation for what Lorraine had done for me. My own fear of Lorraine's death had caused me to drop out of the picture when she needed me most. It would take years before I would shed the burden of guilt.

Whenever I came to South Bend, I attempted to see all four nieces and one nephew. I began getting to know Jim and found him surprisingly easy to talk with. There were places where his life's experiences mirrored my own. In 1948, the same year I was born, Jim's father Frank deserted his wife and eleven-year-old son. Suddenly, Bernadette was faced with raising her son on her own. She determined that no matter what, her son would get the best education available to him. She set her sights on Loyola Academy, a Catholic college prep school for boys.

"I would have been fine in a public high school but Mother would have none of it," Jim used to say.

His mother's goal could not be realized on the lone salary of a secretary. Jim would have to work. He started out with odd jobs after school; then he took on a paper route. At thirteen, he toted buckets of coal door-to-door. At fifteen, with the help of an uncle, he landed a summer job in construction and returned to it each year while he was in high school. All the while he remained on the honor roll.

A photograph taken when he was a senior reveals a handsome face with a trace of a smile on thin lips and a crown of thick blond hair. Anyone looking at the picture would have thought him one of the most popular fellows in the class. But long work hours followed by studying left little time for socializing. When Jim spoke about that period of his young life, he admitted without any bitterness that he never felt comfortable inviting friends to their apartment.

"We had no money to buy living room furniture. Putting money aside for my tuition was Mother's top priority. I had very few dates during high school. I never felt that I belonged at Loyola Academy in the first place."

The commitment and hard work of mother and son paid off. Upon graduation from high school, Jim received a scholarship to Loyola University, Chicago. This was the first step toward a career that would make him known around the world.

Jim and I shared our disappointments; we confided in one another our own shortcomings, including a propensity for making bad choices in our personal lives. In many ways we were the cause of our own pain. Sometimes we'd just sit on his sofa and listen to music. We took his daughters, my nieces, to the beach. At least once we brought Lorraine's youngest daughter along with us. On such ventures I imagined the five of us as a family. Jim was doing the same. It was a relief when he finally said the words.

"How would you feel about moving here and making a life with the girls and me?" It wasn't exactly the dream proposal, but we had already done that with other people. I would be turning thirty-two in a few months and he, forty-three. We had seen enough of life to know that there are no perfect situations. But we thought we saw an opportunity to make things better for all of us. That was May. On August 12, 1980, we stood in a judge's chamber and made our commitments. The judge's secretary dutifully signed on the line as our only witness.

For different reasons, Jim and I were unsure if marriage would work. I had never considered the ramifications of even dating outside my own race, much less marriage. His reputation at Notre Dame and beyond was daunting. I had only a high school diploma and a semester or two of classes at a community college. Jim did not consider either my race or lack of education to be a problem. He had the attitude that the people who mattered to him would accept me and the rest didn't matter. We each had doubts about our ability to sustain a marriage for the long haul.

We discussed our uncertainties and agreed not to tell anyone, even his daughters, for at least six months just in case it didn't work out. I delayed changing my surname until we felt sure that the marriage wasn't a mistake. The arrangement was unusual and would impact all of us, especially his daughters, my nieces. They were nine and eleven years old and should have been included in the conversations about our plans to become a family.

Would we do it this way again? I hope not. But that is how we started our journey together.

I asked Jim if I could bring my sister Lorraine's youngest child to live with us. Without hesitation, he said "yes." I did not ask to add Lorraine's sixteen-year-old daughter nor her thirteen-year-old son to our blended household. That

CHAPTER 9

My Husband, My Friend

There were moments during our first six months of marriage that I thought, "Well, you could say it isn't working and walk away."

My years of apartment living with other single women in no way prepared me to run a home or to play the role of mother to three young girls. Yet, there I was trying to do it anyway. Jim's intuition picked up on my concerns before I got the nerve to share them with him.

"If you don't think you can do this," he said one evening, "I would prefer you go before the girls get too used to your being here. Maybe it's selfish of me, but I want this to work more than I realized. I think we can do it, but only if we are both in equally. *In for a penny, in for a pound.*"

In due time I would come to understand the full meaning of that little saying. Jim did not half do anything. When he made a commitment to do something, whether it was washing all the windows on a given Saturday or making sure his daughters had a stable home, he gave the effort his all. No holding back.

His determination and true grit approach to the task we had taken on as a couple were what kept me holding on even when I felt incompetent at everything except for my job. I still flew for United Airlines. When it was time to go to work, I sometimes left him almost literally "holding the bag" of groceries waiting to be unpacked and put away or of laundry that seemed to reproduce while we were asleep.

Like his mother, Jim looked years younger than his age. He was just under 5'11" and weighed around 185 pounds. He reminded me of 50s movie star, Tab Hunter. Though no one was stopping him for autographs, he was handsome in that clean-cut kind of way. But it wasn't his looks that captured my heart. It was the moments we shared together.

Jim loved movies. We spent many evenings snuggled together on a quilt in front of a cozy fire eating popcorn and re-watching some of our favorites. During our life together, Jim and I must have seen *A Man for All Seasons* at least a dozen times. Set in 16th century England, the story tells of Sir Thomas More's refusal to compromise his integrity even in the face of losing everything that was dear to him, including his fortune, his family, and his own life. I often though how much alike they were: Sir Thomas, a martyr for his ideals, and my husband, a Don Quixote of flawless moral courage. It wouldn't have surprised me if he, too, sacrificed all he had for justice. His character radiated integrity.

Jim was the only running partner I ever had. We started most of our days with a quick two-mile run up to campus and back. Once in a while, we might even do three but no more than that. At first I felt awkward, but it did not take long for me to get used to—and even enjoy—his company on those early morning jogs. We used to hold hands as we walked the last block or two. Jim, ever the gentleman, always took the outside nearest the traffic as his mother had taught him to do when he was a kid. He opened doors and pulled out chairs for ladies. The people I loved growing up in the rural South would have appreciated these simple gestures. They were part of his nature and another reason for loving him.

That isn't to say that we never had a fight during our twenty-two years together. The biggest one started out with a four-mile walk around one of the two lakes on campus. We knew before ever leaving home that there was a chance of a summer thunderstorm. But we looked at the sky and gambled that we had at least an hour of dry afternoon left.

With less than a mile to go, Jim looked at the sky and realized that the rain was upon us. He suggested that we stop in the University Club and have a cold beer and an appetizer while waiting for the storm to pass. I argued that we were not dressed properly. Instead, we should step up our pace and continue on home.

"Okay. As you wish," he said, his words followed by silence. Within five minutes the skies split wide open and rain came down in buckets. With the University Club now a few blocks behind us, there was no place to take shelter.

Without a word, my husband, the gentleman, took off running as fast as he could. I was stunned. I couldn't believe what had just happened. I alternately walked and ran the last three blocks home. When I arrived, he was in the shower. I could feel the anger rising as I peeled off my soaked pants and stepped out of them leaving them on the bedroom floor. The second he opened the bathroom door, I began yelling.

"How could you do that to me? You left me behind and never looked back. What is wrong with you?"

Jim had already dried off and pulled on a pair of pants. He continued blow-drying his hair, paying no attention to my ranting. He turned off the blow dryer and calmly put it in the basket under the sink where we always kept it. All the while I fumed. He stepped around me and started down the stairs. I wanted to strangle him or hit him hard with a skillet. The only thing within reach was a handful of bobby pins falling from my drooping French roll. I yanked them out of my tangled hair and threw them as hard as I could toward his naked torso and face. He stomped down the stairs away from my fury.

Looking down, I realized I was naked except for the

cold, wet t-shirt clinging to my tired body. Once in the bathroom, I closed the door and finished undressing. The surge of water from the showerhead triggered tears of waning anger. My eyes stung as I released them freely while soft, warm water soothed the rest of me. By the time I wrapped myself in the oversized bath towel, my anger had died. The momentary feeling of shame for my poor behavior nearly caused another eruption, but my sudden eagerness to be near him dominated everything else.

Hasty footsteps signaled my coming before I reached the landing. He stood up from his favorite chair as I entered the room; our words collided in the space between us.

"I'm sorry," we said at the same time. Hugging each other as if one of us had finally returned from a long absence, I smiled into the warmth of his neck.

The first and only time we went camping, Jim did everything from prepping the food we would eat to laying out the tent in the backyard to check it for holes. He left nothing to chance. When we arrived at a state park, we all helped to set up the tent. The girls could barely contain their excitement. Though I had not protested in front of them, I was less than enthusiastic about the whole sleeping outdoors thing.

The sounds of the night got to me. Jim tried to assure me that the rustling around outside was nothing more than a raccoon and that the tent was designed to prevent it from getting in. Knowing that he had taken every precaution to make sure we were all safe, I tried to find comfort in his words, but I was unable to convince myself.

The plan was to spend two nights before returning home on Sunday afternoon, but on Saturday morning, right after breakfast, we packed up and left. It was a quiet ride.

Everyone except me nursed feelings of disappointment and anger. By dinnertime on Sunday, they had forgiven me for dragging us back to our air-conditioned house, a house equipped with toilets that did not require an escort in the middle of the night.

A year or two later, Jim came up with an idea. "Let's fly to Salt Lake City and take Amtrak back to Denver," he said during an evening stroll. He had driven from Indiana to Colorado long before the girls were born. Occasionally he remembered aloud the beauty of the Rockies. "The girls will get a better view of the landscape from ground level rather than flying over it," he continued.

"That sounds good to me. I love trains. Let's do it."

The girls were delighted. The trip went without a hitch. Once we got off the train in Denver, we rented a car and drove two hours to a Dude Ranch we had researched online. For four full days, the girls rode horses, helped build campfires, hiked, and practiced roping the stationary bull. This time no one asked to leave early.

We chose Hawaii as the destination for our last family vacation. By then the girls were old enough to go off on their own. The Pacific Ocean was a five-minute walk from our hotel entrance, and the girls were great swimmers. Thirty years later those days in Hawaii stand out as among the best that our family shared.

Two years into our marriage, at age thirty-four, I was diagnosed with early stage cervical cancer. The doctors suggested a hysterectomy, but they spared me chemo and radiation. Four years later I developed fibrocystic breast disease. It is not life threatening, only troublesome. Because of my sister Lorraine's history, for the next five years I was screened every six months for possible cancer and underwent multiple lumpectomies and biopsies.

Jim went with me to Indianapolis to a specialist three times before she referred me to a teaching specialist at the University of Chicago Hospital. We made that trip together at least a dozen times. In spite of how busy he was, my husband rearranged his schedule to spend those days with me. At the end of each visit, he gave me a special treat. Sometimes it was lunch in a restaurant he had checked out ahead of time.

Nordstrom's is my favorite place to shop for shoes because they always have a nice selection to fit my size 10 narrow feet. As much as Jim hated shopping, there were days when he would say, "We have some time. Do you want to go to Nordstrom's?"

Man oh man, how I wanted to say, "Yes, yes. Let's go." I knew that the venture would add at least another two hours to an already long day.

"No," I'd say. "Not this time, but thanks so much for being willing. I can get to Nordstrom's when I'm on a San Francisco or a Seattle layover. Let's go home."

Once, when I had been called back for a second biopsy, he went all out and got us a room at The Drake in Chicago and had them order fresh flowers. The cost of one night there would have fed our family for a month. Once in the room he told me, "I figured that if the news were bad, we would spend the night holding each other in the luxury of a king-sized bed. If it were good, we'd do the same thing—but with Champagne."

We drank Champagne.

Nights at four and five star hotels were not the norm for us, but Jim made certain that they were not so rare as to seem like brand new experiences each time we checked in. We drove our cars until they were old, and we did not belong to country clubs. But when we traveled, he loved staying in fine hotels.

At home our social life was uncomplicated. We hosted countless dinner parties and accepted invitations to even more. For the most part, I took care of buying and preparing the food after we decided the menu together. Jim,

God bless his soul, cleaned up behind me as I chopped and stirred and seasoned large pots of gumbo or roasted a leg of lamb or prepared his favorite veal dish, osso bucco.

Had you been a guest on a given night, you might have found yourself seated opposite a postal worker, an elementary or high school teacher, a college security officer, or Jim's mentor, world famous physicist, Max Dresden, who was a close friend of Nobel Prize winner Enrico Fermi. A full Professor of Physics at Notre Dame, Jim sat at the head of the table; I, a former sharecropper, sat at the other end. In those early days, I half expected someone to walk in and reprimand me back to the kitchen.

CHAPTER 10

9-11

The most unforgettable thing to happen to me during my thirty-one years as a flight attendant was being in the air on 911. Our non-stop flight from Tokyo had been bound for Chicago. With seven hours remaining, the captain informed the chief purser that we would be landing in Anchorage. She then relayed his cryptic report first to several members tucked away in the forward galley and later to the remainder of us in the back of the airplane. The fact that she read from notes she had taken when he called her to the cockpit meant that the captain had instructed her to write down what he said and read it back to him before speaking to her crew.

"The captain has just informed me that there has been a general threat against some of America's commercial aircraft and we are going to have an unscheduled landing in Anchorage. We are to act as if everything is normal, and by no means are we to give our passengers any cause for alarm."

About an hour later the captain made an announcement over the PA that the FAA had diverted our flight and we would be landing in Alaska before going on to Chicago. His exact words are lost to me now, but I remember how natural he made it sound.

For the second time, the chief purser gathered half the crew in the first class galley while the rest of us remained visible in the aisles carrying out our duties. This time her report included the news about the twin towers. After speaking with the first group, she made her way to the very back of the 747 jumbo jet. Too nervous to sit, I was standing in front of my favorite jump seat. The flight attendant assigned the door opposite mine had a daughter living in New York. When she heard the report, she collapsed into a heap on the floor and had to be revived.

By the time we were in range of Anchorage, that airport was crammed with unscheduled aircraft that the FAA forced to land. At that point the purser was summoned back to the cockpit and given a final update that included the new destination, Fairbanks.

Once we landed and the engines were shut down, the captain came over the public address system and explained what had happened. For at least a minute, it seemed that the more than three hundred people on board simply froze. No one spoke or cried out. Then there came a rush of audible gasps, intermittent sobbing, and a flurry of questions seemingly from everyone at the same time.

My husband was again in London, England, on sabbatical. United ground personnel brought cell phones to the crew while we were still onboard with our distressed passengers. No overseas calls were allowed. That being the case, I telephoned a friend in Indiana and had him contact Jim to say that I was safe.

It would still be a few hours before we reached the hotels that, in some cases, had re-opened to accommodate hundreds of unexpected guests. Once in the lobby, passengers and crew alike stood around like zombies with all eyes glued to the television screen. No one seemed in a hurry to get to individual rooms. Instead, we watched over and over the same replays of the actual aircraft being flown at high speed into the giant skyscrapers.

We spent three full days in Fairbanks, and for the first two I did not shed a single tear. Worried I had lost all feeling for humanity, I called my pastor for spiritual guidance. He assured me that in time my grief and sorrow would come. When I did begin crying that third morning, I wondered if I would ever stop.

Our 747 aircraft was among the first flights to arrive at O'Hare after the attack. It was about 9:30 p.m., and all any of us wanted to do was to get to our own homes and families. In keeping with decorum, the crew deplaned last. When we reached the end of the jetway and set foot into the gate room, we were greeted by a large band of our co-workers, most in uniform.

That night we were all one family as mechanics, cabin service, customer service agents, supervisors, pilots, and flight attendants formed a mass choir and chanted: "You are safe; you are safe." Their words reopened the floodgates for some, including me. As my eyes made contact with a sea of faces, I thought to myself, "But what about those who did not return safe?

CHAPTER 11

The Day
Everything Changed

It was a dreary Thursday morning the last time I saw him alive—the last week in March. The calendar told my eyes that spring had arrived several days earlier, but the piercing wind that greeted me as I walked from our house to the garage said that winter was holding on. Northern Indiana is known for its tough winters with excessive snowfalls. The light dusting beneath my feet reminded me to pay attention where I stepped. One misplaced foot could send me plummeting downward to the concrete walkway.

It was difficult to distinguish the powdery flakes from frost. I wanted no part of either. Already, my mind was speeding toward returning home on Easter Sunday to spend the day with my husband Jim and close friends. We had talked about renting a movie and watching it in bed before going to Jerry and Fran's for dinner. It would be just the four of us.

The alarm clock was set for 7:30 but I had gotten up before it violated the soft quietness of our bedroom. I slipped from beneath the covers and into the shower without disturbing him. The water felt good and I spent a few extra minutes enjoying its warmth on my back. Frequently Jim and I enjoyed the closeness of showering together, but not that morning. There was no need for him to be up. We discussed his plans for the day the night before. That was normal for us.

He had an 11 o'clock doctor's appointment before heading to his office in the Physics Department at Notre Dame. Later in the afternoon, he would sit in on a class that was being taught by a trusted colleague and friend. Jim had begun the semester teaching the small class of five graduate students. A recent bout with depression, coupled with his belief that he was going into dementia, led him to the decision to step back and have someone else complete the six remaining weeks.

One of his colleagues graciously agreed to do so and had taught only two sessions when Jim sent him an e-mail saying that, if it was okay, he would like to come and sit in on some of the classes which took place on Thursday afternoons. His friend was delighted at this turn of events and took it as a sign that his long-time friend was feeling better. Perhaps the anti-depressants combined with counseling and the love and support of family and close friends was working. Maybe Jim would even change his mind about retiring the following year. Besides, none of those qualified to assess his performance saw any signs of dementia. However, the only opinion that mattered in that regard was his, and he remained convinced that he was headed down a slippery slope from which there would be no return.

I got dressed in the bathroom, taking care to do so as quietly as possible. Our bedroom was just across the hall. I had planned on waking Jim to say goodbye, but to my surprise when I came out of the bathroom, the bedroom door was open and he was standing at the foot of the bed near the dresser. I hugged him good morning and suggested he go back to bed.

"You don't have to be anywhere until 11 o'clock. Why don't you try and sleep a little longer. I'll come up and see you before I go."

"I think I'll do that," he said, vigorously scratching his scalp with both hands as he sometimes did. I had no idea that those were the last words I would ever hear him speak. I can't erase the picture of him standing there so close to me and yet already in another place, somewhere out of view from those he would leave behind. I watched as he crawled back into bed and burrowed under the covers.

I left the room closing the door behind me and descended the hardwood stairs as quietly as they would permit. There were two or three places between the landing and the bottom step that creaked. After almost twenty-two years in the same house, I invariably landed on those steps when trying not to disturb anyone who might be asleep upstairs.

I had a light breakfast and then said my prayers. I had been using a technique suggested in a recent sermon I'd listened to on tape. The pastor—not mine—had proposed that in order to pray effectively, one needed to pray *the word* and in order to pray it appropriately, it had to be *written on the heart.* She went on to say that reading scriptures into my cassette player and then listening to the recording as you are falling asleep is an excellent way to memorize scripture.

I had filled one side of a sixty-minute cassette with scriptures and was working on the other. The Bible verses led me into my own prayer. That week I was praying for healing for my husband as well as for the safety of a family who was living out a dream by hiking the Machu Picchu trail in Peru. They were among Jim's dearest friends; when I married him, they became the same to me.

Early in our marriage, Jim told me he had three and a half close friends. Actually, there were a total of seven individuals, but he counted each married couple as a unit; a priest made up the half.

When I went back upstairs to say goodbye, I found him sleeping peacefully. At least that is what I thought at the time. I considered kissing him lightly on the cheek but decided against it. Why disturb him? Later I wondered if he had been lying still counting the seconds until he could get out of bed and move about freely, knowing that he would have the house to himself for three days. Looking at him from the doorway, I whispered, "I love you," before gently closing the door for the second time that morning. He could sleep another two hours and still easily make the late morning appointment.

Once in my car and headed for the airport, my mind shifted to my job. I would be working my favorite trip to Japan, but first I had to take the twenty-minute flight on a small plane from South Bend across Lake Michigan to O'Hare airport. I parked my car in one of the spaces designated for flight crew and made my way across the lot to the terminal. Leaning forward into the gusting wind, I thought about the short but almost assuredly bumpy flight ahead. As a thirty-year veteran flight attendant, I had never worked on anything smaller than jets accommodating a hundred passengers or more. The largest, and my personal favorite, the Boeing 747, had a capacity of just fewer than four hundred seats. That was the airplane I would be on later that day.

As it turned out, the flight was delayed. I had, of course, factored in that possibility the night before. Commuters who want to preserve their jobs have at least one backup plan. I was luckier than most of my peers because one of my options was a bus service that could be relied on in all but the severest of weather. I slept for most of the ride, as did my friend Larry, another flight attendant who also lived in South Bend and who would be on the To-kyo flight with me. Had we been lucky enough to fly from South Bend to Chicago, we would have gotten to work two hours before check-in time. Instead, we stepped off the bus fifteen minutes before we were due in briefing.

O'Hare was, and remains to this day, a second home. Except for the hundreds of travelers with their carts, roller bags, and bundles, I could almost maneuver my way blind-folded from one concourse to another.

United flight 881 was scheduled to depart at one o'clock. Shortly before the agent was to close the airplane door, I got off and went into the boarding area to call Jim. I thought I might catch him at his office and ask how the appointment had gone with the doctor. I felt no sense of alarm whatsoever when he did not answer. I figured that he was at lunch with one of his faithful three and a half. I got back on board. Twelve hours later the non-stop flight landed at Narita International Airport. Chicago (ORD) to Narita (NRT) had been my route of choice for at least two years.

I preferred trips to Asia over any of the European flying that was available. My first choice was Hong Kong, but my seniority did not usually allow me to hold that trip on the days I wanted. Now and then I would throw in a month of Beijing flights. I had worked it two or three times and had even taken Jim with me the preceding summer. We'd had fun sightseeing with some of my flying partners. Several of us went shopping, and he bought me a beautiful strand of pearls that back home appraised for more than three times what he paid. Throughout our marriage, Jim never with-held anything that he thought would make me happy.

When Larry and I, along with fifteen more flight attendants, reached our layover hotel, I went directly to my room, wrote a note, and faxed it to Jim. That had been my routine countless times in the past. The thirteen-hour time difference meant that the fax machine in the office of the Physics Department would receive the transmission before daylight on Good Friday. Jim would come in around nine o'clock that morning, and one of the secretaries would have put the note in his mailbox. Of course, as he was reading it, I would probably be asleep.

I always woke up two or three hours after retiring no matter how tired I was when I went to bed. The bright red glow of the message light meant that a response to my fax had been received, and one of the nice bell staff would have slipped it under my door. But that early morning, which was now the Saturday before Easter, there was no red light.

I calculated the time again in my head and decided

that maybe he was going in a bit later. Telephone calls from the Tokyu Hotel to the States were relatively inexpensive, and we sometimes communicated that way.[1] I called home first and then his office, but got no response either place. Still not overly concerned, I turned out the light and tried to go back to sleep but could not.

After reaching only voice mail on my second round of calls, I felt the first inkling of apprehension. I called Barbara and asked her to go over to see if Jim's car was in the garage and, if so, to please ring the doorbell. Barbara and I chose one another as sisters in the early 80s after her girls had already claimed me as their aunt.

"Of course, I'll go over and see what's going on as soon as I get dressed."

It was only after I called the doctor's office to ask whether or not Jim had reported for his appointment that I became legitimately frightened. The receptionist said that not only had he not come for the appointment, he had also not called to cancel or reschedule. Jim would never be that inconsiderate. Something was terribly wrong. I called Barbara back and told her what I had just learned and suggested that she take her husband with her. The past three months had been difficult for my husband, but lately he had shown marked signs of improvement. Still, I knew

---

[1] United Airlines had a contract with the Tokyu Hotel (yes, that's how they spell it), located in Narita, Japan. Crew-members went there for long layovers before flying back to the States.

that something wasn't right.

A few minutes later, I dialed my home number and Barbara answered. She said they had just entered the house and called out but had gotten no response even though Jim's car was in the garage. I stayed on the phone with her—both of us silent as her husband climbed the stairs to investigate. The sound of his voice sent slivers of ice through my body.

"Get off the phone," I heard him yell, "and call 911!"

"Wait! Tell me what is going on."

"Nimbi, I have to get off the phone and call the police.

I am so sorry. He is gone."

I dropped the telephone that had been my lifeline for the past several minutes and clutched at the collar of my nightshirt. Without warning, it had begun choking me to the point that breathing was difficult. I don't know why the security guard was not summoned as I ran screaming down the hotel hallway. At least one couple opened their door enough to poke their heads out trying to determine if there was a fire or some other dangerous situation that threatened their safety. What they saw instead was a tall, seemingly deranged black woman running and calling out a name that meant nothing to them.

My friend Maureen was several rooms down the hall, and I instinctively ran in that direction. My shouting must have terrified her as she had been sleeping soundly, her heart pounding just as hard as were my fists beating against the door. When she opened it, I collapsed into her unsteady body, nearly taking us both to the floor.

She told me later that initially she could not understand my rambling and kept asking me to slow down and tell her what the matter was. When I got the words out one at a time, she immediately began calling on God to help us. I followed her lead instinctively and dropped to my knees.

Desperate to have some contact with Jim, with what was happening around him, I called my home number a second time. When my sister Barbara answered, I asked her to ask Enzo if Jim looked peaceful lying there in bed.

"Nimbi, he didn't die in bed." "How did he do it?"

"I'm so sorry. He hanged himself."

Maureen told me later that I screamed and dropped the phone. She grabbed the receiver and asked my sister, "What did you say to her?"

"I told her how he died. What happened?" Maureen answered, "She fainted."

Maureen called another friend and crew member, Lucas, and told him to come immediately. I don't know where his room was in relation to hers, but it seemed he got to us in no time. For the next twelve hours, Lucas and Maureen became my primary caretakers. They made all of the arrangements for me to fly home on the next available flight, regardless of airline. The numbness in my legs became apparent when I tried to stand after having sat on the side of Maureen's bed for some time. She and Lucas got me back to my room, then called Larry and Toshiko, both good friends of mine.

Larry knew Jim well; Toshiko and my husband had met at least three times. We had visited her home in Chicago, and she had come to ours with her husband and granddaughter. Jim knew that all of these special people would be on my flight. If his mind was allowing any rational thoughts to filter in during those final days, he may have taken comfort knowing that, if notified of his death while at work, I would be surrounded by people who were more than just flying partners.

One of the most grievous outcomes of suicide is that there are no answers to questions that come at you like a raging waterfall. When had he known that he would do this thing? Was he planning it when I hugged him that last time or did he get up and, instead of getting dressed for the doctor's appointment, decide that he had no desire or reason to go on? Didn't he know that I would have gone with him on his one-way journey?

A few years earlier we read a newspaper article about an elderly couple, perhaps in their eighties, who one day walked out into Lake Michigan hand-in-hand until they disappeared. We agreed at the time that, for them, it had probably been a lovely way to die. The article had said they were married more than sixty years.

By the time Jim and I married, both my parents and one sister were already dead. On occasion I reminded him that he must never leave me but rather allow me to be the first to go. Had it been within his power, I know that he would have done what I asked. In the end, the final decision was not his. I believe that a silent foe had been at work within him far too long—one that he was powerless against.

The kind, caring man I loved and who loved me would never knowingly do anything that would cause pain to anyone—especially the unending hurt that is inextricably connected to suicide. But such a point for consideration would have required a rational line of reasoning. Suicide, one therapist told me, by its very nature is an irrational act carried out by an otherwise rational person. My husband did not choose suicide—it chose him. Death by hanging is said to occur within a few seconds—one, one thousand, two one thousand, three...

I pray it took no longer.

****

Flight attendants carry more drugs than any one of us would ever use. This is because we have learned to anticipate the need for them before it arises. Flying international flights, we had easy access to medicines that would require prescriptions in the States. Pills for pain, sleeping, diet and birth control are as common in our bags as toothbrushes and deodorant. There is nothing illegal about purchasing them at legitimate pharmacies in Asia, South America, and Europe. You simply walk in and ask for what you want. Thus, when I had been crying uncontrollably for a long time, one of my friends urged me to take a couple of Valium to calm me down.

Prior to slipping into that uneasy, medicated state, scenes from my life with Jim prodded their way into my consciousness. For more than two decades I had been the wife of a prominent scholar who was known in many parts of the world for his work in theoretical physics and the philosophy of science. I had gone with him when he had been among the invited guest speakers in Brazil, Germany, Italy, Spain, and Sweden. Jim taught in Notre Dame's London program and took two sabbaticals in Cambridge, England, giving us the opportunity to live in another country. Such a life would have been a dream for almost anyone, but given my beginnings, it was nothing short of a miracle that I wound up with such an incredible man. How would I go on without him?

When it was time to leave Japan and return home, Toshiko insisted on accompanying me. Doing so meant about three hundred dollars less pay since she would not be completing her assigned trip. Refusing to keep to her original schedule, she went with me to the airport.

United had booked us two seats on a Japan Airlines

flight that arrived in Chicago four hours sooner than our own. Toshiko's first language is Japanese. Once we were onboard and settled in our seats, she pulled aside one of the flight attendants and spoke to her softly in their language.

I imagine that she told them only what they needed to know, which seemed to include that she would tell them if we needed anything. I know that food was placed in front of us and also water. She kept reminding me to drink water. We were both crying and holding hands for the first hour or so and then on and off again as our emotions dictated. At some point, I told her how grateful I was that she had made the sacrifice to return home with me. Her reply was that she loved Jim too, and she knew that, if our situations were reversed, I would have done the same for her.

At the end of the long flight, we received special attention that got us to the front of the line in customs. Once in the huge meeting area, I had no trouble spotting four of the three and half waiting with open arms. We drove back to South Bend. The next few hours are no longer clear as to the sequence of events. I believe that I asked to be taken home before going to the funeral parlor.

By choice, I entered the house alone hoping to get some sense of Jim's spirit. I wasn't sure what to expect other than that he would not be there. The house was cold, no doubt due to his having turned the heat down to transform our home into a personal morgue. Slowly I climbed the stairs, oblivious to whether or not there was a squeak. Everything was still and there was an aura of the whole house having been sanitized. I did not detect a scent of any kind—not from the fireplace nor the kitchen nor the bathroom. Had everything been wiped clean or I had lost one or more of my senses?

There was no need to be careful about entering the bedroom, and yet I realized that I was tiptoeing about just as I had two mornings ago. The bed was made and nothing was out of place. I stripped myself naked, turned back the covers, and lay in the spot where I'd last seen him. The cold sheets on my skin were a relief. It told me that at least my sense of touch was still working. The tears that had come up to that point were anguished and hard, unlike those that I cried into his pillow. This act marked the true beginning of the long journey still to come. How and why had this awful thing happened to the two of us?

CHAPTER 12

Beauty for Ashes

My husband's death did more than shake my foundation. It dismantled it completely. As sometimes happens between couples that are married for a long time, there were situations when Jim and I didn't need verbal communication. A certain look or gesture spoke the answer to an unspoken question. We knew each other's strengths and challenges. Jim did all the hard stuff—not just physical chores. He made sure we were on track with our finances.

I was happy to come within $100 of balancing my monthly checking account; he balanced to the penny every time. We could have paid someone to prepare our tax returns, but most years he did them. Now, I would have to take care of such practical details. If there was a how-to book to help me get through the day-by-day rituals of life without him, I wasn't aware of it.

For at least three days before the service was to take place, family members came to the house and camped out.

I welcomed the sounds of their voices and the movement of their footsteps coming and going. Their crying accompanied my own, and at times we made an odd sounding choir when aching sobs overlapped between rooms.

Late on the night before we would all gather at the church to say farewell, one of my nieces arrived with her three young children. They had driven seven hours from St. Louis. Her act of kindness and compassion left me speechless.

When Shirley Moore died in 1993, those of us who had shared the same apartment and, more importantly, Shirley's friendship, made a pact to meet at least once a year in her memory. Now, those friends had come to offer me their love and support. We call ourselves Reunion Sisters, and that is how we think of one another—sisters, not friends. Dee Dee, Deborah, Patricia, Sylvia, Tresa, and Lois, had flown in from California. Niki and Lynda made the ninety-minute drive from Chicago.

On the morning of the memorial service, the church was packed. When it came my turn to speak, my eyes searched for the cluster of women who meant so much to me. I could almost feel them willing me to stay strong. As I began reading from the pages I had printed the night before, I reminded myself to stay focused on the faces of those gathered. I gasped at the sight of a second group of flying friends. Two of them, Maureen and Lucas, had been with me in Japan when I got the news of Jim's death.

I have a number of longtime friends extending from my early 20s to today. The bond I share with flight attendants, though, is unlike any other. The nature of our work sets a stage for lasting friendships. Over many years, we share our personal lives with one another having never eaten a single meal in the other's home. Within our group we use a term called *jump seat therapy* that works like this: Sitting side-by-side on a fold-down seat designed not for comfort but for safety, we hear about Kate's first day at school. It seems only a short while later that we are looking at pictures of her walking down the aisle on her father's arm. We share the pain of failing marriages and get to know spouses we'll never meet. Given the intimacy of relationships built over countless ocean crossings and discovering new cities and cultures together, it is no wonder that the alliances we build often last for a lifetime.

My sister Rosemarie had seldom left my side since driving from Columbus, Ohio, several hours after I'd gotten home from Japan. That morning was no different. In the days that followed, after everyone else had returned to their homes, Sis made sure that I remembered to eat from the abundance of food friends had carried in as well as to drink water and to nap whenever I could. She removed the phone from the bedroom with an admonishment: "If I can't get to the phones downstairs, let the machine answer."

In the early stages of my grief there was no way to track or anticipate my emotions. The book of Psalms teems with prayers for every imaginable circumstance. It became my most useful spiritual tool. In chapter 30, it is written that *weeping may last for a night but joy comes in the morning.* Elsewhere in the scriptures, God reminds us that His time is not like ours. In this instance, His night crawled on for weeks. The cover of darkness did bring with it a strange sort of comfort. When alone in my bed, I wept into the softness of my pillow until my eyes had no more tears. Psalm 56 says that God sees our tossing in the night and catches our every tear and stores them in a jar. How long would it take, I wondered, before my jar overflowed?

I had cried at the loss of my grandmother, three siblings, and a few friends. Wailing, however, was new to me. It swept over me like a tidal wave for which I was unprepared. The first time it happened, I was home alone doing a load of wash in the basement. Without realizing it, I shifted my body against the washer. The churning motion of the machine matched that within my stomach and the sensation to heave up my insides was overwhelming, but nothing came.

I moved to another section of the basement. There, in semi-darkness, I sprawled out on my back like a giant-sized rag doll on an air mattress someone had used the night before. My mouth opened to release a long high-pitched squeal that must have been building since the phone call in that hotel room. Then came another and another. It was the middle of the afternoon, and I prayed that the walls around me were thick enough to conceal my agony from the neighbors. When the awful sounds decreased to whimpers and then to shallow breathing, I felt a sense of relief. *That was horrible, but at least it is over. The worst of the mourning is over.* I was wrong. It had only begun.

My calendar hardly ever had a blank page. Notes reminding me of meetings, dental appointments, lunch and dinner invitations and, of course, my flight schedule, were written in various colors of ink depending on which pen I grabbed at the time. Weeks earlier I had volunteered to help with a fundraiser pancake breakfast. It never occurred to me to cancel. No one would have batted an eye given that Jim's memorial service had taken place only four days earlier. In desperate need of distraction, I thought that for a couple of hours I might succeed in diverting my attention from my burden of sadness to almost anything else. For at least two hours, I could flip pancakes or place two on a plate before handing it off to the next lady who would add the bacon or sausage.

A heartbreak of the magnitude of Jim's death is difficult to describe and impossible to comprehend. As selfless and unassuming as he was, his colleagues and friends in academia viewed him as irreplaceable. That sentiment radiated even stronger within our intimate group of friends. Jim had etched an indelible mark in our minds and hearts.

While everyone showed me tremendous compassion and tenderness, they were dealing with their own hurt and confusion. Life did not stop for any of us. At the same time, it offered no plan of escape from the abyss into which we had been hurled.

Without telling me, my sister—my real sister—had been positioning herself to move to South Bend temporarily. With the help of a good friend she had worked with in the past, Sis landed a job before quitting the one she enjoyed in Columbus. Putting my well-being above all else, she pulled up stakes and moved in with me for sixteen months. Rosemarie Harris is her name, and she walked with me both in the literal and figurative sense until I could stand on my own.

I had been in counseling off and on for ten years.

Now it became part of my weekly regimen, and my therapist became my friend. She insisted that in addition to our weekly sessions, I would benefit from joining a suicide support group. Doris made the necessary phone calls and one day, when I stood up to leave her office, she gave me a card with the information I needed in order to make the next meeting.

That experience proved to be more helpful than I could have imagined. One of the four women in the group was the trained counselor and facilitator. Her teenage child had taken his life. There were also three men: One had found his wife in their garage; another still grieved for a twin who had shot himself years before; the last one told the story of his grown son putting a handgun to his head after losing a high paying job. As the newcomer on that first evening, I said little more than my first name followed by, "My husband was the victim."

The need to find the right words or inflections on those words was lifted as soon as we all sat down together in comfortable chairs around a table; I finally felt understood. For three months, I looked forward to and, at the same time, dreaded Wednesday evenings. Those who were farther along on the journey consistently reminded me that in time, "It will get better."

One night a young woman came in with a peculiar problem. She had been considering suicide for almost a year. Her story gripped all of our attention because of the detached way that she told it. She relayed events in minute detail but in a manner that almost made it seem she was talking about someone else. Through that young woman's sharing, I got a close-up view of the torment that Jim must have borne.

"My parents are old and I am their only child. I know that if I end my own life, in a way, I will be ending theirs too."

She hoped that by witnessing the suffering of survivors like those of us in the meetings, she would be able to go on living without causing that kind of anguish for her parents. To be sure, this was an unorthodox situation, but nobody questioned her right to be present. After three or four meetings, she stopped coming. Because of the anonymity in the way the sessions were conducted, there was no way to find out what happened to her. I searched the obituaries for the next two weeks hoping not to see a picture of her pretty, gaunt face.

Jim died in March. Three months later I returned to work. My flying partners were both kind and sensitive without being intrusive. Once on the airplane, I relaxed and returned to the groove of doing what had come naturally for almost thirty years. I had considered the pros and cons of returning to Japan so soon. In the end, that was the flight I chose to work. When it was over and my crew and I had been driven to the hotel, I wondered about the wisdom of my choice. Maybe I should have worked domestic trips for a month or two, I thought. I would just have to make the best of it.

It was impossible to return to the Tokyu Hotel without reliving some of the horrors of the last time I had been there. I requested a room in a different part of the building from where I had preferred staying on my other trips. I had chosen the older section because those rooms had two beds and I liked the freedom of spreading all of my stuff on the extra bed. But now it seemed smart to go to the newer wing.

There was no note to write and fax to Jim. No red light blinked on my phone to signal that a fax from him had been slipped under my door. The forty-eight hours went by slowly. The heartache demanded my attention but no more than when I was home where everything reminded me of him. I had always loved flying. If I could tap back into the rhythm of being on twelve and fifteen-hour non-stop flights doing what came as second nature to me, I stood a good chance of surviving.

When not at work, another band of women were constants in my life. Before Rosemarie returned to Columbus, Ohio, she helped me to move from the house that at different times had been home for each of us. Jim had died there. The memories, both sweet and sorrowful, filled every corner. Perhaps a neutral setting, a home that I had not shared with anyone, might help me to heal. I struck gold.

Loretta lived directly across the street and was the first to welcome me to the neighborhood. In no time at all, we became friends of the type that exchanged keys to each other's homes. More than anything, I think I missed the sense of touch—not sensual, but of simply being hugged. There were times when I would call and ask if I could just come over for a hug. She always obliged.

Before moving, I frequently abandoned the bed and trudged my way down the stairs to Jim's small study. With my back pressed firmly against the back of the sofa, I mimicked the sensation of being snuggled up next to him. We had called that position 'spooning.' I slept for two to three hours like that. When in bed, I made a trench in the middle by lining pillows up in front and in back of me and repeated another verse from Psalms, chapter 139. "I have hemmed you in behind and before. I have laid my hand upon you." Whispering that verse over and over, I felt surrounded by the loving arms of Jesus and began sleeping for as long as four hours at a time.

People gave me an assortment of books. Some I found more helpful than others. A cousin of Jim's hit the mark when he sent me *No Time to Say Goodbye – Surviving the Suicide of a Loved One* by Carla Fine. I don't think I had met Michael more than twice, but somehow he had made the right choice. I kept that book on or near my nightstand for months as my "go to" practical resource of choice. The author writes with sensitivity and honesty as a survivor whose husband also took his life. I could relate to her story as she described the heartache, shame, guilt, anger, and loneliness that are unavoidable after such loss.

Ms. Fine cited numerous cases of others who walked the same road and were willing to share their stories in hopes of helping themselves and others. She pulls back the cloak of darkness that society has wrapped around suicide as a way to avoid dealing with something that is both unnatural and uncomfortable to speak about in public.

This book let me know that I was not alone, and there was hope that life could go on.

Three years had gone by without Jim when I received the following email from my chosen sister, Barbara. There have been many, but this one stands out for it is filled with hope. It came in response to a letter I had written to Jim and shared with her.

Tuesday, May 31, 2005

Little Sister,

This letter is stunningly beautiful, a tribute to love and courage. You tell Jim that he no longer thinks of you, but I believe that love, like water and air, circulates, changes form, and returns; it is never lost. Your love for Jim and your prayers, your trust that the Father would take care of him – all of these are engraved in God's heart where he honors our confidence in His infinite mercy. He has said that He has prepared many mansions for those who believe. I trust that He knows that your eternal dwelling place would be incomplete without Jim in it. The alternatives of Hell and Paradise are not the only ones open to us, Nimbi. For those of loving heart and tortured ideals, there must be a place of pondering, of sorting, of accepting, of learning to know what we were unable to accept by faith alone. At last, when He is ready to call you, you will find your greatest love waiting for you in the peace of eternal forgiveness, rest, and joy.

Barbara

Four years to the day after Jim left us, my first and only grandchild was born. Paulo Santiago Garcia is legally my great-nephew. His mother, Pamela Odom Garcia, is the daughter of my oldest sister, Lorraine Harris Odom, who died when Pam was eleven. Pam is the niece that Jim welcomed to our family. A few months into her pregnancy, she asked me if I would be the grandmother of her child. Of course, I was thrilled.

When the time came for her to deliver, I was in San Antonio with Pam and her husband. They wanted both grandmothers present for the birth. I stood beside her bed and alternated between holding her hand, wiping her face with a cool cloth, and praying while she pushed her baby boy into the world. Paulo was born on the same date, March 28th, as my husband had died four years earlier.

God sometimes gives us beauty for ashes. That is the only explanation I have to offer for such a miracle as this.

CHAPTER 11

Precious Lord,
Take My Hand

Hard work and tragedy combined may have been the glue that held my family together. If true, then mine is no different from many, if not most, families of my generation.

My sharecropping parents escaped the rigors of that life in 1948 by migrating North from the miniscule town of Eads, Tennessee, to Saint Louis, Missouri. They had five children at that time, ages seventeen to eight years. It was necessary for everyone who was old enough to work to do just that. Upon arriving in Saint Louis, the family of seven lived in a basement apartment that Daddy had rented for himself a few months earlier. Growing up in such close surroundings had its advantages. For Jonathan and Landers, the environment helped to forge a bond between them that intensified with time and circumstance.

My mother had given birth to two girls. The first died in

infancy. The second, Lorraine, thrived, and was succeeded by a string of five brothers; one of these also died as a baby. Lorraine, the oldest of all the children, was already a talented seamstress, having been taught by our grandmother. As a high school senior, she continued studying that craft and landed a job in a small dress shop. In her free time she repaired and altered garments for friends and neighbors on the antiquated, foot pedal Singer sewing machine. It had been one of the few household items Mama insisted on transporting to the new home.

A savvy businessman hired two of my brothers as shine boys to work in his downtown parlor. At fifteen and thirteen, Jonathan and Landers were energetic and accustomed to hard work. They were also tall, polite, good-looking, friendly young men. Indeed, they possessed all the qualities necessary for that or most any job dealing with the public. But colored people did not have a wide range of occupational opportunities back then. While Missouri was, in some ways, more liberal than Tennessee, segregation still showed its pockmarked face in the "colored" and "white" signs plastered on doors of public restrooms and second-rate eating establishments.

It no longer surprises me that neither of my brothers looks back on that era of their lives as having been particularly harsh. They say with a shrug, "That's just the way things were." They had, they say, no choice. Colored people did what was needed in order to survive as long as it was honest; that stipulation was non-negotiable as far as our parents were concerned.

The four brothers that lived were close, but in later years the special link between Jonathan and Landers was evident to anyone who knew them. They had a common name for each other. Jonathan used it routinely. Exactly when the use of *Homes* replaced their given names is not clear. However, it was understood that the nickname was something between the two of them. When Jonathan spoke of his younger brother to the rest of us, it was, "Landers did" or "Landers said." But when speaking brother to brother, the name each used for the other was *Homes*.

For at least the last ten years of his life, Landers was laden with a list of infirmities from his brain to his feet, with failing kidneys being the main complaint. Fifty years ago, he began drinking fine bourbons and cognacs often and generally late into the night. At the same time, the southern cuisine he grew up eating on Sundays and holidays became the regular fare. Church's fried chicken, grease dripping barbecue sandwiches from The Rib Shack, and sweet potato pies were some if his very favorite foods.

The only exercise he did on a regular basis was standing to cheer his Saint Louis Cardinals. Given all that, it is no wonder that at seventy-seven his body rebelled against the years of abuse it had tolerated.

When Landers, the younger Homes, moved to Sioux Falls, South Dakota, in the 90s, I was stunned.

"Why on earth did you choose that place? Look around you. How many black people do you see?" I asked.

My brother laughed. "Yeah, you may be right. But I like Sioux Falls and, once the word gets out that I'm here, watch out. *They* will come in flocks."

What happened instead was the people of Sioux Falls embraced him in a way that could not have been foreseen. The same magic he had wielded over our family all his life touched everyone with whom he came in contact.

Growing older has its rewards, and my brother's life experiences molded him into a rare form of gentleman. Blessed with good looks, a radiant sense of humor and a style unique to himself, he was a magnet that pulled in all sorts of people. His closet was filled with fine suits, oversized hats, and a dozen pair of $500 cowboy boots. Landers became part of the fabric of a city and culture he grew to love. The natives were helpless against such a gentle, strong force of a man. They had no choice but to adopt him as their own.

Beleaguered with kidney malfunction for more than a decade, in the spring of 2012, he underwent a second open-heart surgery. The mini strokes that followed would prove to be his ultimate opponent. A two-month stay at a nursing/rehab facility ended when he said, "Enough."

He stood defiant against the appeals from his two children and both sisters, so we called in the big gun. But not even the other Homes was able to convince Landers to remain and receive the care physicians said he desperately needed. On a summer afternoon in June, he simply checked himself out, called his buddy, Norm, and asked to be taken home. There my brother began a new life on his terms.

He was able to manage living alone due to the faithfulness of his dear friend Stacey. Young enough to be his daughter, she called him Pops. Three times a week she stopped by and counted out a collection of capsules and pills aimed to treat all his ills. The cigar box sized, light blue, plastic pillbox had become the centerpiece on his kitchen table. A few weeks into the new routine, in one of our frequent phone conversations, Landers seemed amazed by Stacey's conscientious support.

"She takes care of my medicines, does my laundry, cleans my apartment, and cooks for me. And she won't let me give her anything, not one dime. I can't believe it."

I was in my car on a back road in Indiana when her call came. I pulled over to the side, turned everything off, and tried to calm her down while trying to snuff out the fear that had ignited in the pit of my own stomach.

"Calm down, Stacey, and tell me what is going on. It's going to be okay."

I needed her to believe my words even if I did not.

She said that she had not been able to reach Landers by phone after several attempts and had gone by his jewelry shop, only to find the closed sign still in place from the day before.

"I came to the apartment but he isn't answering the door and the chain is still latched. His car is in the space he always leaves it."

My brother had two cars. He referred to the one he used daily as The Lemon. The Lemon was a yellow 1991 Cadillac. At the time it had 135,000 miles on it. He bought it for $1500 and drove it for two years before it was hit by a truck and declared totaled by the insurance company. It was the other driver's fault. The insurance company paid book value, a hundred dollars more than my brother had paid for it.

With $1600 cash in his pocket, he took the car to the second hand dealership where he had bought it, Don's Auto Repair and Sales, and asked if they could just make it drivable. According to him, Don took a large hammer to the passenger side of the car and pummeled hanging pieces of metal back into place—more or less. The end result was a car with two out of four doors permanently nailed shut, a windshield that looks like the back of Spider Man's suit, and a trunk that springs open without warning as if Jimmy Hoffa is trying to kick his way out.

I had visited him a month before Stacey's call. He was

in need of a driver due to cataract surgery, and I was it. The experience turned out to be one splattered with jokes and funny stories. My brother tried to convince me that it was perfectly okay to put what I viewed as a death trap on the freeway.

"We only have to go five or six exits and we will miss all the traffic lights."

"Not on your life." I told him through tears of laughter. "You may be crazy enough to do that, but not me. That windshield will fly in on us as soon as we head into the wind."

"But Don is the Lemon King, and I have his guarantee that that windshield will hold steady. I drive it on the freeway all the time."

I knew that he was telling me the truth. He must have had a guardian angel always at his side. I wouldn't venture to guess how many of those angels applied for early retirement after a stint with him.

I asked Stacey to see if the second car was in the garage. She said that it was.

"Okay. Listen to me. Do not enter the apartment.
Call Galen and then dial 911."

Galen Stoops was my brother's closest friend. Well into his eighties and suffering from congestive heart failure, he found walking even a few feet to be a challenge. His poor health did not keep Galen from visiting Landers at his shop several times a week. That afternoon in response to Stacey's call, he arrived at my brother's apartment with his son Rick about the same time as the police.

I remained on the phone and could hear the officer alternately asking questions of Stacey and calling for my brother to open the door.

"We're going to have to break the chain."

I cautioned Stacey to stay in the hallway but, against my recommendation, she followed the officer inside, as did Galen. For a few seconds I could hear nothing over her screams. I disconnected from her cell phone and dialed Galen. He was not much better. I yelled at him to please give his phone to the police officer.

"Is my brother alive?" I asked, in a surprisingly calm tone.

"He is breathing but unresponsive. It looks like he might have passed out and hit his head on the floor. An ambulance has already been summoned."

Seconds later the paramedics were shouting orders for everyone to get out of the way. I imagined them lifting his unconscious six foot six, two hundred pound body onto a gurney and speeding toward the hospital. Stacey told me that she would follow the ambulance and call me once they got there.

"I will come as soon as possible, but the last flight of the day has already departed."

The following morning while it was still dark, I set out for South Dakota. The first leg of the trip was a three-hour bus ride from my home in Indiana to O'Hare Airport. An hour later, it was a relief to strap myself into a seat for the ninety-minute non-stop flight to Sioux Falls. The desire for sleep disappeared soon after my seat partner sat down and offered a friendly greeting.

Neverlyn Johnson, an affable black woman of my generation, was making a surprise visit to see her ten-year-old granddaughter perform in a school play that evening.

The jubilant grandmother would then return to her home in Bear, Delaware, the following day.

She is even nuttier than my brother Landers, I thought. *How many blacks are there in all of Delaware, not to mention a town called Bear?*

Having just met the woman, I did not voice the question but instead recounted to her the conversation I had with Landers when he moved to Sioux Falls. Neverlyn told me that she had lived in Sioux Falls and still had family there. She then invited me to join her for lunch. I explained that I had to get to Sanford Hospital as soon as possible. But just out of curiosity, I asked, "Where are you having lunch?"

"Minerva's." She answered.

"What a coincidence. That is right down the street from my brother's jewelry shop."

"What is the name of the shop?"

"Eye Catching Jewelry." I replied, almost breathless with anticipation of her next words.

"Oh my goodness! I know your brother. He has re-paired several pieces of jewelry for me, and my husband bought a bracelet from him."

Stacey was waiting for me when I stepped outside the airport. We went straight to the hospital. By the time I reached him, Landers had been in critical care unit number 2302 for nineteen hours. The feeling that he would not be leaving gnawed at the edge of my gut.

Though Death was stamped all over my brother, from the countless wires of various colors that grew out of his gauze wrapped head to the pulsating boot-like apparatus that hugged his legs and feet, the Grim Reaper took his time in coming. Landers' face and right eye were noticeably swollen, presumably from the fall. A patch of raw skin the size of my palm marred his shoulder like an ugly tattoo.

I had seen him immediately after open-heart surgery, but even that image was not as frightening as the picture now before me. Within thirty-six hours, five more family members made their way to the hospital and joined me in the vigil.

One day melted into the next during which time Jonathan made intermittent appeals for someone to read a chapter in the reflexology book that had become his Bible of sorts. Unlike Landers, Jonathan for the past forty years had followed a healthy diet enhanced by regular exercise. He was convinced that it was still not too late to save his last brother. More than once he touched Landers' arm or hand and said, "You are going to make it, Homes. You are going to make it."

Jonathan urged me almost pleadingly to help him massage Landers' feet. He was convinced that if we squeezed, pressed and kneaded that part of the foot connected to the kidneys, our brother would wake up.

Preposterous? Of course. But the love on Jonathan's face and the desperation in his eyes washed me in shame for having felt annoyance at his insistence for help in this final ritual.

"I need someone to help me because both feet have to be massaged at the same time."

We stood, shoulder-to-shoulder, at the foot of the deathbed. Jonathan held Landers' right foot and I, his left. I tried to imitate and synchronize the movement of my hands to those of my brother—soon to be my only brother. My hands grew tired but I continued the exercise and stopped only after Jonathan gently let go of our brother's swollen limb, then lowered his head and left the room without saying a word.

After countless conversations and briefings with now

faceless physicians, Landers' two children, Elinor and Dorian, were ready to let their dad go. Jonathan, Rosemarie, and I agreed with their decision. We had already lost three siblings. The onslaught of painful emotions that crowded in on us were not new. Still, it was our first experience in all being present at the bedside of a dying brother. We drew strength from one another like three interwoven branches on a single tree.

I contacted the nurse and advised her of our decision. Within a few minutes, three more attendants arrived. One of them, a young, dark haired man, spoke to us in a calm voice and explained in detail what they were about to do. As kind and sensitive as they all seemed, without meaning to, I had tagged them as the Death Squad the instant they entered the room. Slowly they began turning off machines before finally pulling the tube from Landers' throat. With a loud exhale, he involuntarily arched his back and attempted to lift his head.

The medical staff had cautioned us that, once all life support systems were stopped, we should be prepared to see our loved one go within minutes. Two days earlier, they had said the process could take hours or days, but things had gone bad quickly and now we were at the end.

Once the respiratory folks exited, the nurse told us that we could not hurt Landers and encouraged us to do whatever we felt comfortable doing. Finally, after days of having been careful not to interfere with the web of tubes, needles and lines crisscrossing his swollen body, we were given free rein. We kissed his face, stroked his arms, rubbed his chest, and clutched his hands while whispering prayers and good wishes into his ears.

Landers lingered. It seemed he wanted to make sure we each had as much time as we needed. We stood by him, sometimes in small clusters and other times alone. Two hours later, Landers was still breathing on his own. Jonathan asked Dorian to take him to a supermarket.

Dorian's wife, Razle, went to rest in a nearby waiting room leaving Elinor, Rosemarie and me in a room that, without the sound of machines, had become as quiet as a tomb.

At one point I said to Landers, "You have just as many on the other side who love you dearly," and proceeded to name them one by one: Big Mama, Granddaddy, Mama, Daddy, Lorraine, Charles, Ed Roy, and on and on.

My brother took his last breath at 4:45 on a Thursday afternoon.

Thirty minutes after Landers died, Jonathan and Dorian returned from an errand that had taken longer than it might have. My hunch is that Homes and Homes were so in sync that Jonathan sensed death was imminent and knew Landers would not want Dorian to witness it. The vigil had been hard for all of us, but for Dorian it seemed almost unbearable. A trip to the store would be long enough for Landers to make his escape. That's what he did.

Earlier that day, two members of the Palliative Care staff had prepped us about what needed to be done once Landers was gone. When asked, Rick Stoops, Galen's son, provided the name of a funeral director. I contacted them soon after we agreed to stop life support. Landers had not left information of any kind that would help in the decisions that now had to be made.

"How did he feel about organ donation?" We asked one another. None of us knew the answer, but we all thought that he probably didn't have anything that could be used.

One of the coordinators of the unit sought me out to ask if the family would be willing to donate his corneas.

Elinor and Dorian said yes. It gave us a momentary lift to learn that death did not have the final say. Because of Landers, two people would have sight. He would have liked that a lot.

None of us was surprised to find that he had no life insurance. The simple truth is that Landers Harris was just too busy living life in a way that nourished everyone who knew him. His last words at the end of every phone conversation were always the same. "Just be happy, y'hear?"

The day after Landers died, his son, daughter-in- law, and two siblings departed for their separate homes. His daughter Elinor and I stayed behind to finalize the closing down of his shop and clearing out his apartment. During the final hour in the apartment, Elinor remembered something she had discovered earlier that would gladden our hearts. "Look at this, TT (her pet name for me); I found this yesterday and kept it out to show you. It was in Daddy's nightstand drawer with a few other things."

She handed me the unfolded yellowing sheet of paper and left the room. When I saw the first line, tears of joy burst from my eyes. My brother had written out the words to an old spiritual we had all grown up hearing our elders sing.

Precious Lord, take my hand; lead me on
    let me stand.
I am tired, I am weak, I am worn;
Through the storm, through the night, lead me on to
    the light.
Take my hand, Precious Lord, lead me home. When
    my way grows drear
Precious Lord, linger near, When my life is almost
    gone, Hear my cry, hear my call, Hold my hand
    lest I fall.
Take my hand, Precious Lord, lead me home. When
    the darkness appears and the night draws near,
 And the day is already past and gone,
At the river bank I stand, guide my feet,
    hold my hand
Take my hand, Precious Lord, lead me home.

By the time I got to the end of that song, I was literally walking through the apartment shouting to the top of my voice. "Thank you, Jesus!" I said, over and over again. I knew in that moment that Landers had a personal relationship with his savior.

As I was leaving Sioux Falls for what was likely the last time, I got another surprise. The United Express gate agents remarked that they had seen me coming and going a lot in the past several weeks.

"Well," I explained. "My brother used to live here but he died two days ago. Yesterday his daughter and I finished clearing out his apartment and his jewelry store."

One of the two looked at me and said, "Oh my goodness. Are you Landers' sister?"

"Yes, I am. Did you know my brother?"

"Yes, I was in his shop more than once. Everyone who met him liked him."

My final trip to his bedside had begun with meeting a stranger who knew him. Now it was ending the same way. Two chance encounters—two gifts of grace.

A week later, the five of us who had spent those last days with Landers gathered with other family members and friends to say our last goodbye. The service lasted little more than an hour. A niece, a nephew, a granddaughter and I took turns at the microphone to share a portion of what Landers Harris had meant to us. Laughter erupted as we told stories about how easy it was to sweet-talk him into doing crazy things. Once he drove his brand new Cadillac over to our brother Ed Roy's house to show it off. Within minutes one of Ed Roy's sons, who had just gotten his driver's license, convinced him to hand over the keys.

One niece observed that while there were more than a dozen of them, "Uncle Landers had a way of making each one of us feel like we were his favorite."

My brother has been gone for a while now but when, on occasion, I stop and listen closely, I can still hear his voice.

"Just be happy, y'hear?

CHAPTER 14

Still Time to Love

I was fifty-three when my husband died. He was a remarkable man in every good sense of that word, who loved and nurtured me in all the ways that matter to a woman—or at least to this woman. Thus, even after my grief had been salved, I felt no sense of urgency to start dating.

After all, I was past my prime and certain needs that might have been relevant at forty were less so as I stared sixty in the face. Still, it was about that time that I began to reflect on how much I missed having a male companion in my life.

Up to that point I had enjoyed fulfilling relationships with several women—two who were also widows, one several years younger and the other the same age as I. We had not previously been intimate friends but found ourselves bound together by circumstance. Linda's husband had died the year before mine. As wife to the associate pastor, she was very visible within our church. I began sitting with her soon after I started coming to church alone. Sherry's husband died after mine. We three widows became pew partners and more. Living near one another made it easy to share impromptu meals, morning walks, and movie nights.

After Jim died, I no longer found it easy to live in the home that held so many memories. I sold the house near the university. I moved into a new neighborhood, to my good fortune, across the street from Loretta. She was divorced and lived alone. We shared many evenings together, more in her home than mine; mostly because I invited myself over.

"Hi, friend, can I come over?" Instead of being annoyed, Loretta welcomed my phone calls.

Sometimes Loretta extended the invitation. "Hey, neighbor. I've got a whole head of cauliflower and a new recipe to try. Want to come over?"

I'd be walking into her front door almost before she hung up the phone. More often than not, the simple meal turned into a feast. The background music punctuated our conversation while she chopped and stirred and I sipped whatever wine we were drinking that night. All in all, life was good. But once I allowed myself to recall how it felt to go out to dinner with a gentleman who held doors open and reached across the table to touch my hand, I began to wish for that part of my life to return. At first I did not acknowledge such feelings to anyone. I felt guilty for having them. Was it too soon and I too old for such things?

When I did voice my inner thought to my friends, I found that I was not the only one experiencing them. But the prospects were grim. I wanted a man of integrity who was kind, considerate, loyal, and who treated me like a lady. The men I knew who possessed such traits were either married or gay. Gay men have proven to be among my most faithful and sensitive friends. They have delivered home-made soup and flowers to my door when I was laid low with a cold or the flu; they have come with their pick-up trucks when I bought a piece of furniture without considering how I'd get it home; and they have lied to me about the way I looked after three days in bed without shampooing my hair or putting on any makeup. But there was still something missing that could only be filled by a relationship with the potential for romance.

I met Jim Langford through unexpected circumstances. Oddly enough his sister Lois and I had lived a few blocks apart for years. She came to my aid in a unique and sensitive way during the early weeks of my grieving after my husband's death. Ten years later I wrote a book and Lois read it. She suggested that I send a copy to her brother.

"He owns a small publishing company and I think he would like your book." I mailed a copy to his home and soon after, he called me.

The sound of his voice over the phone ignited sensations that I had forgotten. He could have been in broadcasting.

The fact that his comments about the book were flattering made his voice even more appealing. I didn't know what to make of the fluttery feeling that lingered long after we hung up.

A week later I drove to his farmhouse. He was recovering from a broken leg and could not easily come out to meet me elsewhere. When I entered the cozy living room, his smile said hello before he even parted his lips/ A single man and a scholar, appearance did not seem to be all that important to him. He wore comfortable loose fitting pants to accommodate his leg. The dark blue sweatshirt sprinkled with toast crumbs left over from breakfast further attested to his relaxed nature. A complete wall, from the hardwood floor almost to the ceiling, was lined with hundreds of books. With a casual wave of his hand, Jim said, after we had been chatting for a few minutes, "These are my friends."

I felt as if I should reply, "Pleased to meet you all." Instead, I smiled.

I liked him immediately and knew that we would become friends. Near the end of my third visit to his place, he said in a charming way, "I think that I am smitten with you." I didn't know it then but, in that moment, he had me. Who says smitten anymore? Not anybody that I knew. It did not take long for him to lure me into the safety of his cocoon with heartfelt words and laughter.

"I have a cat named Dawg," Jim said one day. "My

daughter Emily decided when I was recovering from cancer that I needed one to keep me company. Even though I reminded her that I hated cats, she brought one here anyway. You won't see her though as she hides whenever anyone comes over."

"Well, that's good," I replied, "because I hate cats too."

However, after a few more evenings together, Jim, his cat, and I became a newer version of *Three's Company*. Though her formal name is Dawg, I refused to call her that—even once. We agreed to call her Dee. In spite of myself, I began having conversations with her from across the room. Before long I found myself at the pet store buying a toy, a tiny pink collar, and a heart shaped identification tag with her name and Jim's phone number on it.

"You'll never get close enough to put that damn thing on her," he stated with assurance. I knew by the smirk on his face that he wanted Dee to scamper away as I approached her.

"Jim, I know that she will allow me to put this on her if you keep out of it. Since you insist on letting her outside, anyone finding her needs to know that she has a home."

In my softest voice I asked Dee's permission to put something around her neck, and she acquiesced. Jim, on the other hand, made an undecipherable growling noise and left the room. From that moment on, Dee and I were friends and he was odd man out.

Two days later she came home with no sign of the collar. Jim seemed all too pleased. The next day, I replaced the lost item, this time with a sparkly green one. Within a few hours, Dee returned a second time without her new jewelry. She still goes outside every single day, but I no longer worry about her getting lost. Our smart girl always makes her way back to us.

Jim and I still make each other laugh at least once a day. We don't analyze it nor do we take such a gift for granted. It just is and we accept it with gratitude.

We learned to know one another by paying attention rather than through stilted conversations about our likes and dislikes. We spent a lot of time together, especially during the first few months. The outcome is a deep mutual love that fills our inner longing for completion.

On those evenings when we sit close together on his sofa, the one that should have been replaced long before I met him, we marvel at how quickly we became an old married couple without even trying. We never applied for a license nor did we have any marriage ceremony. In our hearts we are husband and wife living apart but spending as much time together as we choose. In some ways we are as different as night and day. For one thing, he is more than just a fan of baseball; he is an authority who has written books on the sport. I, on the other hand, struggle to keep the team names matched to the appropriate sport.

After Jim, Landers knew more about baseball than anyone I ever met. He died before getting the opportunity to meet Jim, but they had lively conversations through me as I sat at the side of his hospital bed.

Landers would be watching a game—any game as long as a ball and bat were involved. I'd be on the phone with Jim giving him an update on my brother's condition. "Stan Musial was the greatest baseball player the Cardinals ever had," Jim said in one of their first indirect phone calls.

"Landers," I repeated, "Who was the Cardinals greatest baseball player of all times?"

He flashed back, "Stan Musial. Everybody knows that." Everybody except me, that is.

Of course the questions became more difficult. Jim would say, "Ask him if he remembers George Altman."

My brother's two-word reply, "First baseman."

My brother had a stroke after his heart attack and I watched him trying struggle to recall the names of friends of many years who came to the hospital to pay him a visit. Somehow, Jim made a connection to a part of his memory that had not suffered the blackout.

The game between two men, both of whom I loved, went on day after day. The master thoughtfully framed questions that could be answered in two or three words— usually the first and last name of some obscure player. I would give anything to have been able to spend a single afternoon in the same room with my "husband" and my brother. They would have gotten along famously.

Now and then I shock Jim—I sometimes call him Ace—by knowing the answer to a Jeopardy question that involves sports. The St. Louis Cardinals is one of the two teams he most hates and one of the two my brother most loved. A few nights ago I heard myself saying, "Bob Uecker," as I passed through the living room in time to catch the end of a question.

"How the hell did you know that?" He asked in astonishment. I explained that my father was a loyal Cardinals fan and had taken me to a few games when Uecker, "a catcher," I added, was at the height of his career. He shook his head, and then turned his attention back to the program. If he were ever a contestant, we'd be rich. The guy spouts off the answer before the question is even completed. It is more than a little irritating. That time, however, I had gotten his attention with an unexpected right answer, about sports of all things.

Happily, we have enough in common that our differences are not obstacles but rather conversation starters as we continue learning about each other. He is writing his autobiography. Now and then he captures my full attention by asking, "You wanna hear what I wrote today?" More often than not I ask that he read the pages to me a second time, particularly if the subject has been about one of his parents.

Though they have both been gone many years, he is still moved to tears when he reads to me about some of his childhood experiences. The family took long summer drives covering hundreds of miles before cars were air- conditioned. Every other summer they went to Mexico City where his father, who had graduated from the University of Notre Dame, studied for and earned advanced degrees at the National University of Mexico. On alternate years, they traveled either to California to visit Jim's paternal grandfather or to Texas where his maternal grandmother and other relatives lived.

The kids had no say in the planning at all. When Jim was a senior in high school he tried without success to convince his parents to allow him to remain behind. He talked about all the advantages of having someone at home to take care of things and, he added, "I'll get a summer job and save money for college." He had been accepted as an incoming freshman at his father's Alma Mater. But his parents saw through the sudden manifestation of responsibility. They knew that for the first time, young Jim was in love and did not want to be separated from his girlfriend.

The whole family made their way to Mexico. The young lovers sent letters back and forth using Jim's dad's address at the university. "Sometimes, my father came home with seven letters for me, all having been written on the same day."

"Wow! I have never written that many letters to anyone in a single day. Do you have any idea where she is now?"

"Not really," he said softly.

"Good," I replied with a grin. "I would not want to have her as my competition." We both laugh out loud at the idea of such an encounter.

Life is full of zigzags, detours, and dead ends. Who is to say that his high school sweetheart won't suddenly pop up on his face book page? If that were to happen I would encourage him to meet her. I imagine that the boy she fell in love with all those years ago would still be recognizable in the man he has become.

I grew into rather than fell in love with Jim by degrees. The process did not take long. He has faced a string of serious physical challenges with no thought of backing down. Jim Langford fears nothing—not even death. He is my hero.

The mirror shows no compassion to anyone. Each morning it reminds me that, "You have found each other in the winter of your years." His hair, the color of snow with streaks of silver garland, is beautiful to me. Except for the skills of my hairdresser, mine would likely match his.

The slowed pace, the morning aches and pains would

suggest that perhaps the mirror has told the truth. But we have claimed that it is autumn, and early on at that.

I was not looking for Jim Langford, but when I made my way down an unfamiliar road, there he stood.

We are not pausing to ask why we have been brought together. Instead, we treat each day as a precious gift. We take pleasure in the simple things such as an unexpected early morning phone call or a joke played or told, usually by him. He is teaching me how to walk a different stride without straining to go faster, and I am learning the meaning of patience and discovering the joy in having someone at my side no matter the gait. What he gets from me is for him to say, and he does so often with matchless eloquence.

The time that remains for us both is a mystery to which only God knows the answer. Autumn is our favorite season and our prayer is that winter will not hasten to make its way to us. Today, in this moment, we are joyfully soaking up God's love. We feel it in the embrace of the sun's rays streaming down through the colorful Indiana trees.

Alice Rogers Crawford "Big Mama."
Maternal grandmother who raised me.

Elbro Crawford "Granddaddy."
Maternal grandfather. Rosemarie and I lived
with him and Big Mama after our mother died.

Otis Harris, my father.
Died at the age of 63, when I was 20.

Rosa Lee Harris, my mother.
Died at age 37, when I was two years old.

Lorraine Harris Odam, my oldest sister, died at the age of 47. I can still feel her love.

Rosemarie Harris, my only living biological sister. She is my most faithful supporter and fan.

My four brothers. Johnathon, wearing the white sweater, is the only one still living..

Charles Williams, my first husband with me in my first "stewardess" uniform. 1972.

James T. Cushing, my second husband, now deceased. Photo taken in Japan, 1966.

James Langford and I met in 2012 as a result of him reading my first book. We've been together ever since.

My nephew Gregg Odom is more like a little brother! For several years he lived with Rosemarie and me when we were with our grandparents.

Leslie Susan Odom Dudley, a special niece and spiritual mentor. The oldest daughter of my sister Lorraine.

Pamela Grace Odom Garcia, my niece, daughter of Lorraine. She chose me to fill the role of maternal grandmother to her son, Paulo Garcia.

Milton Charles Odom, youngest son of my sister Lorraine. He is a miracle man!

In 2013 while performing his job as a cab driver, he was shot twice in the head at close range. His brain was not touched. Today he is completely well!

Paulo Garcia. my beloved grandson.

Chris Cushing, loving niece, who became my step-daughter in 1980. She located the poem that appears in this book. Chris is the daughter of my sister Rosemarie Hassis.

Ron Harris, son of my brother Ed Roy Harris. At one time we were both flight attendants for United Airlines.

Reverend William and Donna Lou Imler. Bill was my pastor when I moved to Indiana in 1980. Over the years, the couple became more like surrogate parents.